Encouraging Physical Activity in Toddlers

Moving Matters Series

Steve Sanders, EdD

Gryphon House

www.gryphonhouse.com

Published by Gryphon House, Inc.
P. O. Box 10, Lewisville, NC 27023
800.638.0928; 877.638.7576 (fax)
Visit us on the web at www.gryphonhouse.com.

Bulk Purchase

Gryphon House books are available for special premiums and sales promotions as well as for fund-raising use. Special editions or book excerpts also can be created to specifications. For details, call 800.638.0928.

Disclaimer

Gryphon House, Inc., cannot be held responsible for damage, mishap, or injury incurred during the use of or because of activities in this book. Appropriate and reasonable caution and adult supervision of children involved in activities and corresponding to the age and capability of each child involved are recommended at all times. Do not leave children unattended at any time. Observe safety and caution at all times.

Library of Congress Cataloging-in-Publication Data

Sanders, Steve (Steve W.)
  Encouraging physical activity in toddlers / by Steve Sanders, EdD.
      pages cm. -- (Moving matters series)
  Includes bibliographical references and index.
  ISBN 978-0-87659-050-8
1. Physical education for children--Study and teaching (Early childhood) 2. Movement, Aesthetics of--Study and teaching (Higher). 3. Early childhood education--Activity programs. 4. Toddlers--Development. I. Title.
  GV443.S194 2015
  613.7083'2--dc23
                              2015009506

Contents

The Importance of
Physical Activity for Toddlers

CHAPTER

1

You are taking a big step to help the toddler in your care by learning about motor skills and ways to support physical activity. Being physically active every day is important for the healthy growth and development of toddlers. In fact, by doing so, you will help provide the movement foundation for the toddler to stay physically active and healthy throughout life.

Our discussion of toddler physical development will include information on the types of motor skills that should be practiced, setting up the activity environment, and providing appropriate skill-development equipment. This book includes ideas for activities that caregivers and parents can participate in with the toddler. Simple and presented in a straightforward way, the activities do not require a lot of equipment.

However, if you do need a toy or equipment item, the discussion will clarify what you need to have on hand. Activities included in this book are fun—you and the toddler are going to have a great time!

As a caregiver or parent, you have an important role in the physical-skill development process. Please keep in mind that the process for toddlers is different because at no time in a child's life will her physical skills change as rapidly as during the toddler years.

Remember that when the toddler begins walking, she has learned only a few other physical skills. She cannot throw a ball and hit a target. She does not know how to jump and land on two feet or kick a ball into a net. She cannot yet walk across a balance beam or dribble a ball. All these skills must be learned. To eventually master these physical skills, the first steps are exposure to what the skills are and exploring and experimenting with what the body can do. These skills will be learned if the toddler has lots of opportunities to have fun with movement.

The toddler will master very few skills during this time. She will not become efficient at jumping, throwing, kicking a ball, striking a ball with a bat, catching, galloping, or skipping. Sometimes the toddler will scream with excitement at her accomplishments; other times she will be frustrated because she is unable to hit the target or kick the ball. The toddler will appear awkward and unable to repeat movements, and every attempt at a skill will look different. When the toddler is playing with a ball, the ball will appear to control the toddler. This is part of the normal process of toddler skill development.

However, the time between learning to walk and becoming a preschooler is extremely important to prepare the toddler for eventually becoming efficient and competent at a variety of physical skills. Don't think of yourself in the traditional role of a teacher trying to make sure the child learns a specific skill to do well on a test—there is no test. The immediate goal is not to help the toddler refine skills so she can throw or jump better. Her physical skills are just emerging—she is learning the basics. Your role is to guide her as you provide the safe environment, appropriate equipment, and time for the toddler to experiment with all the new movements that she can do with her body. Learning as a toddler is all about exploration and understanding how the world (including the toddler's body) works.

Adults do not have to be athletes or have high levels of physical skills to help the toddler acquire a foundation of basic motor skills. Your role is to be involved, to play with the toddler every day, to be a model, and to provide opportunities for discovery and practice. These opportunities help connect a toddler's muscles and brain and move her toward becoming

efficient and competent in her physical skills through the preschool and elementary years. Experience and research show that toddlers who lack appropriate practice and miss exploring and experimenting with what their bodies can do will later struggle to be competent in physical skills.

Toddlers Are on the Move

Parents and caregivers must understand that learning basic physical skills such as jumping, kicking, throwing, rolling, and balancing takes a lot of effort for toddlers. Their love for physical activity will help them learn many new movements. As their skills improve, they will begin to throw and kick balls, strike balls into the air, walk up and down stairs, run, and even pedal tricycles. They may attempt to do forward rolls and stand on their heads. Practically every item in the cabinet or center—from pots and pans to wooden blocks—will become a musical instrument that the toddler will want to drum and bang.

Physical skills during the toddler years are mostly acquired through unstructured play. To promote this type of practice, you can provide a safe environment with appropriate activities and equipment and then supervise, by being available in the background when needed.

Encouraging Physical Activity in Toddlers

Structured play is also important. That is when you can introduce a toddler to a new piece of equipment, modeling what the item can be used for and then practicing the activity a few times before standing back to let the child explore or to jointly play with the item. For example, roll a ball back and forth between you and the toddler.

Because toddlers' attention spans are short, two to three minutes will be long enough for most activities, unless the toddler is really fascinated. During structured play, reduce the number of distractions and put everything away so you have an uncluttered space for moving around. With unstructured play, you can get out several items and let the child move back and forth between activities as he desires.

When you spend time with toddlers, you will see that there is not much of a line between structured and unstructured play. For instance, the toddler might be climbing freely on a playground structure at the park, and then get stuck and be unable to climb down. In a situation like that, play can quickly become structured as you move closer and guide the placement of his hands and feet so he can climb down to safety.

As you provide structure for a toddler's physical activity, keep in mind that children this age require only small amounts of information to get them moving. Sometimes just rolling a ball to the child will be enough to get him started. Or you might send a beach ball into the air with your hands and say, "Hit it this way." That could be all the structured guidance necessary to get the exploration and learning under way. Too much information can overload even the most interested toddler. At this stage in physical development, it may be better to provide too little information than to provide too much.

Physical-Activity Guidelines

So, you wonder, how much physical activity does a toddler need each day? If the child is going to be physically active throughout life, she must develop a foundation of the necessary skills. Children who do not develop a solid foundation tend to be the ones sitting on the sidelines. Think of it like learning to read: Successful readers are those children who learn the alphabet, how letters can be placed together into words, and how words form sentences. Those who do not master these basic skills may have difficulty learning to read and may not enjoy it as much. Enjoyment of physical activity depends on establishing a base of skills.

If a toddler's home and care environments promote activity and skill development, then she will more likely become competent in a variety of physical activities. In 2009, the National Association for Sport and Physical Education (NASPE)—now called Shape America—published guidelines advising that toddlers should do the following:

- Engage in a total of at least thirty minutes of structured physical activity daily.
- Spend at least sixty minutes—and up to several hours—per day engaged in unstructured physical activity and not be sedentary for more than sixty minutes at a time, except when sleeping.
- Have plenty of opportunities to develop movement skills that will serve as the building blocks for future physical activity.

TODDLERS AND PHYSICAL DISABILITIES

If you think a toddler may have a physical disability, certainly check with her doctor for advice. Be aware, however, that children with disabilities will go through the same developmental progression—although some may be slower—as children without disabilities. The activities discussed in this book show caregivers and parents how to make play time and physical activity a constructive experience for all toddlers.

- Have access to indoor and outdoor areas that meet or exceed recommended safety standards for performing large-muscle activities.
- Have the support of caregivers who promote movement skills by providing opportunities for structured and unstructured physical activity and movement experiences.

As you introduce children to new activities, make sure the equipment you use is always safe and age appropriate.

Guidelines tend to provide minimums, and ideally you will go beyond those minimums. Strive for having toddlers accumulate at least three hours of physical activity at any intensity, spread throughout the day. So have the child participate in short spurts from five minutes to thirty minutes several times each day. Some activity periods may be very physical with lots of running and movement. Other times could involve calmer activities, such as walking on a beam, rolling a ball back and forth, or stacking blocks and knocking them down. Activities can involve a playgroup or family members; opportunities can be found at child care, at the park, or out in the community. The more daily physical play time the toddler gets, the greater the benefits.

What might thirty minutes of structured play look like for you and the toddler? Structured physical activity includes the times when you guide or direct toddlers to learn something new about a physical skill or about a piece of equipment—whenever adults are playing directly with the toddlers. Activities might include modeling how the toddler can lift her feet to climb stairs, swing her arms forward when jumping, play a musical instrument such as a drum or shaker, strike a foam ball with a paddle, walk on a balance beam, or kick a ball.

What might sixty minutes and up to several hours of daily unstructured physical activity look like for a toddler? Unstructured physical activity occurs any time a toddler is playing and exploring her environment on her own. This does not mean that caregivers and parents are not included; adults certainly need to be close by and available for support or playing alongside the toddlers. But unstructured play requires that the toddler is in charge, initiates and leads the activities, and makes all the decisions. Unstructured play might include playing and climbing on the playground, digging in the sandbox, building with blocks, pushing and pulling toys,

Encouraging Physical Activity in Toddlers

The human body has more than 600 muscles, and during the next several years, a toddler will learn to use all of them. By the end of the toddler years, a child will have increased his muscular strength and endurance. Strong muscles assist in controlling posture and balance, learning new physical skills, and reaching developmental milestones.

running and chasing, jumping, or playing with balls. It also gives toddlers a chance to practice skills introduced during structured time.

Motor-Skill Development

A toddler's body is growing fast, and you will often see daily changes in growth and physical skills. Toddlers are different sizes and shapes, and some develop motor skills more quickly than others, but all have the potential to develop a solid foundation of physical skills.

Much of the toddler's day will be spent exploring his environment and learning what his body can do. Toddlers experiment with balancing, throwing, kicking, and striking objects. They climb on everything—including learning to climb stairs—and marvel that they can jump and propel themselves off the ground. Although toddlers will not demonstrate the mature form of any of these skills, they are building their foundation. Exploring and manipulating the environment and learning new physical skills will consume a majority of the toddler's time.

Motor development can be divided into a discussion about fine motor skills and gross motor skills. Children develop fine motor skills to control the movement of the small muscles of the body, specifically in their hands and fingers. Fine motor skills for toddlers include drawing—such as on paper with crayons or on a chalkboard with chalk—putting together jigsaw puzzles, stacking blocks, and using spoons and forks at mealtime. A toddler's developing vision is directly related to learning fine motor skills.

We will discuss fine motor skills in more detail in the section on tracking skills.

Gross motor skills are the movements a toddler learns to control the large muscles of the body, including those in the arms, legs, and feet.

These help toddlers begin to control their bodies and manipulate their environment and include walking, running, climbing, jumping, rolling, kicking, throwing, catching, striking, and learning to ride a tricycle. The toddler years are an introduction to physical skills; children will work on refining their motor skills for many years. Most experts agree that the foundation of gross motor skills in children typically is learned by about age six. After that, children are refining their motor-skill patterns to be more efficient.

To get a sense of the fast growth children undergo from starting to walk to age three, look at the average one-year-old, who weighs about 22 pounds and stands 29 inches tall. By age two, the average toddler weighs 27 pounds and is about 33 inches tall. By age three, he is 30 pounds and 37 inches tall. The development of physical skills occurs rapidly at this time mostly because toddlers now have increased mobility.

To add to this growth, a toddler's teeth begin to appear, which allows him to eat more complex food requiring more chewing to digest. The addition of meat and other proteins into a toddler's diet comes at a time when muscles are getting stronger because of increased physical activity.

Fine motor skills also develop at a fast pace, and toddlers begin to do more detailed tasks using the muscles in their hands and fingers. Caregivers and parents should be aware of the safety concerns that fine motor development brings. Toddlers can now pick up unsafe items from the floor and place them in their mouths; therefore, any small item becomes a potential choking hazard.

Make the toddler's food count. The recommended number of daily calories for a toddler is 1,000 to 1,300. This is not a lot of food but is enough calories for the physical growth and increased physical activity of toddlers. Calories taken into the body must equal calories that are used up during physical activity and normal growth; otherwise, the toddler will gain unwanted weight. Make these calories count by providing as much healthy food as possible. Don't add unneeded calories with foods that are high in sugar. Eating a variety of healthy foods as a toddler is the best way to establish good eating habits that will continue throughout life.

Increased fine motor control enables toddlers to do fun and interesting things such as drawing, stacking blocks, and manipulating a variety of toys. During this time, increased fine motor development lets a toddler to learn to turn pages in a book, begin to feed himself with a spoon, undress himself, and eventually drink from a cup. The toddler will also experiment with a lot of things that can get him into trouble, such as opening cabinets, turning knobs, flipping switches, and generally getting into everything. If you have not already done so, toddler-proof every room. It is important to stay aware of where the toddler is in the environment and what he is doing.

A developmental milestone is a skill toddlers acquire within a specific time frame. For example, developmental milestones for toddlers include walking up and down steps, kicking a ball, throwing a ball overhand, walking backward, and fine motor skills such as threading large beads onto a string and drawing a straight line on a piece of paper.

Developmental Milestones

Toddlers develop physical skills in a specific and predictable sequence, but the rate at which one toddler reaches developmental milestones likely will differ from others her age. There is a range of factors, from genetics to the physical-activity environment, that affects when a toddler will perform certain skills. Toddlers who are more physically active and have an activity-rich environment tend to reach developmental milestones before less active children.

Here are a few physical milestones to watch for with toddlers.

At eighteen months, most toddlers can demonstrate the following gross motor skills:

- Walking alone
- Crawling up steps or possibly walking up steps with help
- Performing an awkward run
- Pulling a toy behind the body while walking
- Standing on one leg with help

If a toddler is not walking by eighteen months, do not be alarmed. This may be normal development for the child, but concerns should be discussed with the child's health-care provider.

At twenty-four months, most toddlers can demonstrate the following gross motor skills:

- Running and then stopping and changing directions without falling
- Kicking a ball forward
- Walking backward
- Leaning over to pick up something without falling
- Pulling and pushing toys
- Sitting down in a small chair
- Walking up and down stairs while holding an adult's hand or railing for support
- Dancing (moving) to music
- Showing interest in jumping by squatting in place as if getting ready to jump

At thirty months, most toddlers can demonstrate the following gross motor skills:

- Jumping in place and frequently falling over when landing
- Galloping
- Throwing a ball overhand
- Threading large beads onto a string
- Copying a horizontal line
- Walking on tiptoes

At thirty-six months, most toddlers can demonstrate the following gross motor skills:

- Riding a tricycle
- Standing briefly on one foot
- Walking up stairs using alternating feet
- Walking down stairs alone, placing both feet on each step
- Jumping with both feet together
- Using tracking skills (although not fully developed, much improved)
- Scribbling with crayons
- Cutting with scissors
- Climbing up and down ladders

Fundamental Movement Skills and Concepts

Physical or motor development, the process by which a child acquires movement patterns and skills, gives children abilities they need to explore and interact with the world of physical activity. Many factors can influence a toddler's motor development, including genetics, body size and build, nutrition, and skill practice.

The research is clear that children develop motor skills during the early childhood years and that those who are not exposed to or instructed in skill-development activities may have slower physical development. A study by Jacqueline Goodway and colleagues found that prekindergarten children with instruction improved their locomotor and object-control skills (for example, running and catching) over children without skill instruction.

Physical Skills

When you help toddlers learn physical skills, you help them fully understand what their bodies can do. Physical-activity skills can be divided into locomotor or traveling skills, balance skills, and manipulative skills. Traveling skills include walking, skipping, galloping, jumping, running, leaping, climbing, hopping, and marching—the skills that help the child get from one place to another. They develop naturally in most children, and by about age eight, most children will have developed the mature forms of hopping, galloping, leaping, and skipping. Demonstrating a mature jumping pattern may take longer to develop for some children.

Unlike traveling skills, balance and manipulative skills, which initially help the toddler move through his environment in a safe way, require much more practice before a child develops a mature form of the skills. Toddlers who can't remain upright and maintain balance when moving tend to get many bumps and bruises. Balance skills include standing, balancing, swinging, stretching, rolling, turning, and bending.

Manipulative skills are related to manipulation of a ball, and the toddler will use them in playing sports or simply playing games for fitness and fun. Manipulative skills include throwing, catching, kicking, striking with body parts as in dribbling a ball, and striking with implements. The toddler will begin practicing all the manipulative skills at about the same time and will continue to refine these skills throughout life, but there is a developmental progression. Children typically develop kicking skills first, then throwing and

FUNDAMENTAL PHYSICAL SKILLS FOR TODDLERS

Although there are other skills that the toddler will be exposed to as he moves through the preschool and adolescent years, the following are basic skills toddlers should explore and practice to provide a foundation of physical development to benefit them for the rest of their lives.

- Traveling skills: walking, skipping, galloping, running, leaping, climbing, hopping, and marching
- Balance skills: standing, balancing, swinging, stretching, jumping, rolling, turning, and bending
- Manipulative skills: throwing, catching, kicking, striking with body parts, and striking with implements

catching skills. Striking with body parts and striking with implements (such as paddles and bats) are normally the last physical skills to develop.

Movement Concepts

In addition to learning basic skills, children should also understand *movement concepts.* These provide specific cognitive information about performing a skill and help children move to higher levels of learning basic skills. Movement concepts enable the child to understand how and where the body can move and the relationships the body has when it is in motion. These concepts also relate to the quality of the movement, describing how a skill should be performed. These are typically not emphasized when working with toddlers. Developmentally, the toddler is not ready to learn about abstract concepts related to space, effort, and relationships. It is appropriate, however, for caregivers and parents to be aware of these concepts so you can present information appropriately when working with the toddler. Concepts are divided into three categories:

- *Space awareness* refers to where the body can move and includes general space, self-space, direction (forward, backward, sideways, diagonally, up, down), pathways (straight, curved, zigzag), and levels (high, middle, low).

- *Effort awareness* includes information on how the body can move and includes the elements of time and force. Consider whether the movement is fast or slow. Is the movement done with force, as when the child strikes a drum hard with a drumstick so it makes a loud noise, or softly, as when the child moves lightly on tiptoes across a room?

- *Relationship awareness* asks the question, "With what or whom can the body move?" This first focuses on the relationship of one body part to another. The child will begin to learn all the parts of the body so he can balance and make body shapes, such as round, narrow, wide, and twisted. It also relates to the interactions with objects (over, under, on, off, near, far, in front of, behind) and other people (leading, following, working with a partner or a group) that the child will have while participating in physical activity.

As you explore the activities in this book, you will see numerous examples of how movement concepts can be used to design practice activities for the child. Using space awareness, for example, you might ask the toddler to strike a ball *high* into the air, walk in a *straight* line, or climb *up* or *down* the stairs. By using these concept words when the child is moving, you will help the toddler begin to understand the meaning of these movement concepts. With toddlers, do not place a lot of emphasis on learning concepts. But there will be a time during the preschool years when knowledge about concepts will help the child refine her physical skills.

A toddler begins learning body parts at about fourteen months of age and will have fun pointing to both your nose and his. (The nose is typically the first body part the toddler can identify.) By the time most toddlers are two, they can point out about ten different body parts. Repeating the names of body parts as the toddler points them out helps him become more aware of his body and what the different parts can do. Just think, learning body parts is the toddler's first anatomy lesson.

Take a few body parts at a time, beginning with the face (nose, mouth, ears, eyes, chin) and then the arms (hands, fingers, elbows) and legs (feet, toes, knees, ankles). Interior body parts (chest, stomach, hips, shoulders, back) are usually the last to be learned. Make learning about body parts fun! Playing body-part games also improves a toddler's verbal development and adds to the number of words he knows. Here are a few body-part activities to try with the toddler:

- Ask the toddler to show you different body parts: "Show me your toes. Now point to my toes."
- Add music and sing a song as you point out different parts. "My head, my shoulders, my knees, my toes . . ."
- Trace the toddler's feet or hands on a piece of paper. Write the names of the body parts on the paper, and draw arrows to the different parts.
- Draw an outline of the toddler's face, and label the parts.
- Ask an older toddler to move different body parts. "Can you wiggle your fingers?" "Can you touch your head with your hand?" "Can you touch your elbow to your knee?"
- Ask an older toddler about body parts. "Which parts help you kick? Which ones help you throw?" Let him show you the part and then do the movement.

Observable Characteristics of Learning Skills

As you play with a toddler and help her develop physical skills, what will you be able to observe about her movement? Children move through similar progressions or levels in learning new skills, and there are observable characteristics at the beginning stages of skill development. Some children travel through the progressions faster than others, and some may not develop their skills to reach the highest level. Development of physical skills is a long process, and it is only natural for children to remain at different levels until practice has improved.

Toddlers begin at the *precontrol stage* of physical development. Remember that toddlers are just learning about physical skills and will lack the ability to control or replicate a movement. For example, if the toddler attempts to kick a ball it may go straight or it may go off to the side. She may kick it with her left foot or with her right. She may attempt to kick and then miss the ball completely when she swings her foot forward to contact the ball. One attempt at kicking the ball will not look like the next. All these actions are normal and to be expected. Parents and caregivers should not expect a toddler to do a skill correctly when she is in the precontrol stage of developing skills.

You may find that the advanced levels (control, utilization, and proficiency) do not apply at this age, as few toddlers will move past the precontrol level. At the *control level,* the child's movements are more consistent and look similar. The child begins to correctly perform the skill more frequently. At the *utilization level,* the child begins using skills in game situations or combining one skill with another (catching a ball and then throwing it, or running to kick a ball into a net with a defender trying to take the ball away). At the last stage, *proficiency,* the skill has become almost automatic. Adolescents and adults who regularly play tennis, compete on a swim team, golf, or play recreational softball have reached the proficient skill level. Of course, professional athletes also have demonstrated proficiency.

Developmentally, toddlers need lots of time to explore, experiment, practice, and repeat movements to move to the control level. Many six-, eight-, and even twelve-year-olds are still at the precontrol level with some skills. Without a good skill foundation and lots of practice and repetition, it is difficult to advance, refine, and improve skills. Age does not determine what level a person has reached. For example, a six-year-old who received lots of practice opportunities to develop balance skills may be at a control or utilization level in balancing. However, because she did not develop a foundation of throwing and catching skills when she was younger, she may still be at the precontrol level at throwing and catching. Many adults are at a precontrol level at several different skills.

Children tend to go through the same observable levels of physical development in learning new skills. Some travel through the stages faster than others, and some advance to higher levels when they have more instruction and practice opportunities. Toddler physical activity is all about establishing a good foundation so that children will have the opportunity to continue to develop and refine their physical skills throughout life.

Strategies to Help Toddlers
Learn Physical Skills

CHAPTER

2

Caring for toddlers is both an exciting and challenging adventure because they are learning at such a fast pace in every area of life. And although they are very active and enthusiastic about exploring, toddlers still have limited physical skills. They fall often, run into objects in their environment, drop toys and cups, spill food, and miss their mouths when attempting to eat. Be patient, and allow toddlers to do things for themselves even though it may be years before they can do tasks consistently and with quality.

One of the most important roles that adults play in a child's development is introducing a toddler to physical skills such as traveling, balance, and climbing skills, along with those related to throwing, catching, kicking, and striking balls. Don't forget fine motor skills, although a toddler will naturally investigate most of these types of activities.

Toddlers' initial learning of physical skills mostly occurs through trial and error, but they need appropriate instruction to become competent. Most toddlers simply are not ready for large amounts of instruction, however. What they need is time to explore and experiment with what their bodies can do. For most toddlers, basic physical skills are learned by lots of practice, exploring, and manipulating equipment, and through observing how others perform skills. The toddler will then imitate and further explore how he can best complete the skill. Your role is to provide the environment and equipment and be available to assist along the way. Sometimes toddlers need adults to play with them, and sometimes they need adults to be in the background observing and just being available. A toddler must travel through this period of exploration and physical maturation before she will be ready for help refining skills.

The two most important ingredients for successful toddler physical activity are a stimulating environment and caregiver involvement. Your role is to participate with the toddler in physical activity regularly and facilitate or guide him. Place the toddler in situations where he can learn by doing. Plan outings to the park, and include activities that involve a range of different physical skills. Provide appropriate equipment, model activities that can be done with the equipment, and then practice the skill with the toddler. When the toddler is ready, move aside so he can explore and practice skills on his own.

Encouraging Physical Activity in Toddlers

When you see that the toddler has questions or is having difficulty with an activity, provide a short demonstration or some words of encouragement. If the toddler is frustrated or simply is not ready to do the skill and be successful, switch activities and return to the activity another time.

Demonstrate that physical activity is something adults and toddlers can enjoy. Toddlers best acquire physical skills—and thinking and social skills—in an environment created for fun! Low-pressure exploration is the key as the child begins a lifelong process of physical-activity learning.

Focus on the skills identified in this book, and plan for daily practice. Without some direction, you might leave important skills out of the routine. For example, one goal might be to emphasize tracking skills four times each week while playing with the toddler. This would suggest that you provide bubble-blowing and beach-ball-striking activities so the child can work on tracking skills. Another goal might be to do activities that involve climbing several times each week or playing with balls every day for twenty minutes. The critical task is to provide time every day for practicing a variety of physical skills. Do not try to practice all important skills every day, but over time, introduce the toddler to and practice all the basic skills. Also, a toddler is too young for emphasis on just one physical skill; all skills need to be explored as often as possible.

While helping toddlers establish a foundation of physical skills, parents and caregivers should remain flexible and observant. The child is not only learning new physical skills but also trying to figure out how the world works. Some strategies may not work as well as others, so keep trying different approaches until you figure out what works best for the toddler.

- Schedule physical activity. A toddler is going to be physically active all on his own throughout the day; in addition, set aside times for specific skill practice to add some needed structure in his daily life.
- Schedule several times throughout the day for physical activity, so the toddler can anticipate and look forward to those times. For example, plan twenty minutes early in the morning and another fifteen minutes before lunch. Go to the park for thirty minutes after nap time and another twenty minutes later in the afternoon. Find a physical-activity

TODDLER CHARACTERISTICS

When you are teaching the toddler about physical skills, remember he is also developing in other areas. Many toddler developmental characteristics will lead to challenging behaviors. Parents and caregivers should set rules or guidelines for toddler play time to provide a safe environment, but they should also avoid being too structured. Relax and enjoy the toddler during this time. Try to understand that the normal toddler characteristics can make this age group fun but can also leave parents and caregivers tired and frustrated.

- Getting into everything and very active; enjoying movement
- Showing curiosity and a drive to explore
- Having short attention spans
- Learning to do things for themselves
- Smiling and laughing at their newfound ability to do physical tasks
- Relying on rituals and routines to provide a sense of control
- Showing a tendency to be easily excited and easily frustrated
- Acting with impulsive behaviors
- Learning to talk and express feelings and ideas
- Demonstrating unpredictability with skills
- Enjoying activities such as building up and knocking down, and putting in and taking out
- Imitating everything they see
- Using the word *no* to demonstrate being assertive and making decisions

playgroup and meet at least one time each week with other toddlers and parents or caregivers.

- Provide the environment and equipment. The toddler needs a place to move and the appropriate equipment to practice developing skills. Play time will be more fun and will benefit the toddler more if the space has been cleared of obstacles and if the child can select from a variety of equipment. Inside or outside, always check the safety of the space before playing. The environment should include storage

for the equipment. Before and after play time, the toddler should participate in getting equipment out and putting equipment away.

● Encourage effort. When children are initially learning new skills, praising for successfully hitting the target or completing a task correctly is not necessary. A majority of the time, the movement will appear awkward and the toddler will not come close to performing the movement correctly. If you focus on evaluating whether the movement is done correctly and then praise the child only when that happens, the toddler is likely to get frustrated. Fun practice, not perfection, is the goal. Encourage participation and effort so toddlers will continue to practice. You might say, "I like that you were able to climb the ladder and slide down the slide. Can you do that again, and can I do it with you?" "Wow, nice job rolling the ball across the ground! Can you roll the ball to me? Then I will roll it back to you." "It is wonderful that you can you jump in the air three times in a row!" Once the toddler is in the preschool years, there will be plenty of time to provide detailed feedback and refine the skills.

● Demonstrate skills. Walk up to a ball on the ground, and kick it hard so that it travels across the playground. Or step up on a log in the woods, and walk across with your arms out to the side. "Look at me—I am balancing!" Many times, you don't have to say a word; just do the activity. The skill really does not need to be done perfectly; the toddler just needs to get the general idea. After watching, the toddler will want to kick the ball and balance on the log just like you.

- Model participation. A toddler will want to repeat and model not only what you do but also your attitude that physical activity is important. You will not send the appropriate message if you get the box of equipment out and then go sit in a lawn chair under a shade tree. You must play and participate in physical activity with the toddler so he will follow your lead.

- Create challenges. If a toddler is consistently able to throw a ball into a basket from three feet away, challenge him to step back and try it from farther away. Start with simple challenges you know he can accomplish; challenges that are too difficult can be frustrating. Parents and caregivers may think that providing feedback to toddlers is not helpful because they may be too involved with the activity to stop and listen. When you provide feedback, make it specific rather than general. It is good for a toddler to hear messages such as, "I like the way you throw the ball," but that will not help him improve the skill. Instead, try, "I like the way you throw the ball! Can you throw it harder?" Not only do you let the toddler know you are watching and interested, but you also provide a challenge that could help improve the skill.

- Get on the toddler's level. Eye contact is critical in getting a toddler to listen to what an adult says, so get face-to-face when communicating about physical activity. Either squat down to his level, or pick him up when talking. You can also sit down next to him and let him describe what he is doing—for instance, how he is filling up the basket with balls.

Creating Healthy Physical-Activity Routines

Encourage daily routines that stimulate good habits such as getting appropriate amounts of sleep, eating healthy foods, and being physically active every day. Practicing healthy habits early can help the toddler develop physical skills and form patterns of behavior that will be beneficial throughout life.

Developmentally appropriate practice simply means that adults take into account the age and experiences of the child and plan learning activities that are appropriate for the developmental age group and for the child as an individual. If a toddler attends a child-care facility, make sure to ask if it has a physical-activity program and if the program is designed using developmentally appropriate guidelines. Physical-activity experiences in child care should be an extension of what families do with toddlers at home. Here are some questions to ask child-care providers if you are looking for a quality physical-activity experience for the toddler:

- Does the facility have safe indoor and outdoor spaces available for daily physical activity? Is there a safe, age-appropriate climbing structure for toddlers?
- Is there enough appropriate equipment for each toddler without needing to wait in a line for a turn? Is equipment lightweight and made for the toddler age group?
- Are both structured and unstructured physical activities planned throughout the day?
- Do staff members use exploration and guided discovery as instructional strategies during physical activity?

For additional information about developmentally appropriate practice related to development of physical skills, see guidelines from the National Association for the Education of Young Children (www. naeyc.org) and from Shape America (www.shapeamerica.org).

For toddlers, older children, and adults, our daily lives are composed of a series of patterns or routines that help us move through the day. For example, most adults have the routine of brushing their teeth several times each day. Some adults stop each morning for a cup of coffee on the way to work, and others may exercise at a local gym on the way home from work.

Establishing a variety of daily routines for the toddler is an important first step to helping her learn about the world. The following are some benefits of routines.

- Security: Consistent routines help children learn to trust adults (at home and at school). When toddlers feel a sense of trust and safety, they are more confident about playing and exploring their world.

- Positive behavior: Routines guide a toddler's action toward a specific goal and can help her learn responsible behavior. For example, the toddler can help you put the blocks back into the storage container when she finishes playing.

- Social skills: Routines such as waving bye-bye help a toddler learn social skills, which will be particularly important in interactions with other children and adults.

- Coping with transitions: Making a transition from one activity to another will be smoother if a toddler has practiced the transition and made it part of her daily routine. A midday routine of lunch, play time, and then a nap will allow the toddler to move through the transitions between these activities without behavior problems.

- Opportunity for learning: Daily routines, such as playing in the backyard, blowing bubbles, listening to music, and kicking a ball—when added to other routine activities such as bath time and reading time—provide wonderful opportunities for you and the toddler to learn about the world and have a great time.

Infants do not really need a routine—they tell adults what they need. They cry, and we feed them when they are hungry. They cry, and we change them when they are wet. The routine parents need most for their infant is sleeping at night. As soon as an infant begins to walk and becomes a toddler, it is time to put some structure in her life and begin to add simple routines to the daily schedule.

Toddler routines can include any activity that is consistently scheduled, such as mealtime, nap time, brushing teeth, play time, time to go to the park, and time to pick up toys. For an activity to become part of the routine, it must consistently occur on most days of the week and at about the same time each day. The child also must practice it regularly.

At times it may work to go with the flow of what the toddler wants to do, but the day will run more smoothly when you establish fun routines. Remember, routines do not have to be boring!

Routines provide two key ingredients for toddlers learning about physical activity—relationships and repetition. One-on-one time between the caregiver and toddler gives the child time to practice physical skills. The more a toddler practices a new physical skill, the better she will get at the skill. Repetition of activities is the foundation of learning. When a toddler knows what is going to happen next, it gives her a sense of security and self-control and she develops a sense of trust of adults, which gives her the opportunity to venture out, explore, and learn about the world.

SLEEP— DID YOU KNOW?

The best way for families to encourage quality sleep for their toddler is to set up a consistent bedtime routine. Structure bedtime events to include a bath, brushing teeth, reading a story, or listening to music. These activities signal the toddler that it is time to relax and sleep. Over time, you may even see the toddler begin to get ready for bed without much help from her parents.

Toddlers love to imitate the behavior of adults in their lives and need adults to be positive role models so that they grow up and make healthy decisions. Parents and caregivers need to make sure they engage in plenty of physical activity to stay healthy. Adults who lead by example and promote healthy eating, sleeping, and physical-activity routines help children develop healthy habits that will remain with them into their own adulthood.

What are other benefits of establishing routines with toddlers?

- You can minimize power struggles. The toddler understands that nap time, play time, brushing teeth, taking a bath, and going to the park all happen at about the same time each day. You don't have to tell the toddler what to do, because the toddler already knows; you simply do the activities together because they are part of the established routine.

- Toddlers learn how to cooperate. When a young child knows what comes next, she does not feel like someone else is making the decision to transition to the next activity for her, so she is less likely to resist.

- The child takes responsibility for her own direction and activities. Toddlers love being in charge of themselves without constant reminders. Routines help young children feel more independent and can reduce arguments with caregivers and parents. When it is time to clean up and do something else, the toddler will understand that the toys need to be picked up before she transitions to the next activity.

- Children learn responsible behavior that keeps them healthy and safe. For example, making it a routine to wash hands before having a snack helps keep everyone safe from germs and sickness. The routine of always holding an adult's hand when crossing the street helps toddlers understand safe behavior.

- Having a schedule will help the toddler fall asleep faster at night.

- The toddler will learn the concept of anticipating what will happen next. She may want to walk down the street to the playground right now, but she can learn that she always goes to the playground after nap time. This practice will give her something to look forward to.

- You will have opportunities to practice physical skills with toddlers every day.
- Toddlers learn the expectations for when things take place. If you assist the toddler in picking up the toys after play time, then she will understand the expectation and, over time, will do the activity without being asked.
- You provide regular opportunities to develop the toddler's social and language skills. For example, during mealtime or play time, toddlers and caregivers can talk to each other, share toys, take turns, and learn to wait. These activities help toddlers develop language skills and other social skills that will help them later in school.

During any one day there may be dozens of short routines you and the toddler might participate in, from mealtime routines to bedtime routines; health and physical activity routines should be added to those. That might include setting aside a time each day (ten to twenty minutes) for skill-development activities (practice jumping, throwing, and kicking); a time to play outside or climb on the playground structure; a time to go for a walk; a time to blow bubbles; a time to pick up and put away toys; a time to listen to and move to music; or a scheduled time for meeting with a playgroup. Also plan daily time for practicing fine motor skills—sit and play with modeling clay or puzzles, draw, or paint. When these kinds of

ROUTINES AND CHILDREN WITH DISABILITIES

You may wonder: What if my child has a disability? Are routines still important? In general, routines are important for all children, including those with different abilities, and physical activity is important for all children. It is best to talk with a health-care provider before the child begins a physical-activity routine. Try to get advice from a professional with experience in physical activity and disabilities. She can tell you more about the amounts and types of physical activity that are appropriate for the child's abilities.

activities are consistently scheduled into the daily routine, a toddler begins to understand that physical activity can be fun and looks forward to it.

Physical-Activity Environment

The physical environments at home and in child care influence the toddler's physical-skill development and lifelong health. Creating an environment that encourages exploration and physical development—one that includes physical-activity equipment; storage for that equipment; an adult acting as a role model; and an open, safe space—is important for children of all ages.

Activity-rich environments will stimulate toddlers' curiosity to experience all the wonderful things their bodies can do. Provide toddlers with opportunities to play and use equipment that allows them to explore the potential of moving and being physically active. Include experiences that allow toddlers to select the activities they will participate in and how long each activity will last, but also include activities that have a clear sequence or pattern and that require toddlers to follow simple adult directions.

A toddler needs a physical-activity environment that is carefully and thoughtfully organized. This does not mean that the environment should always be neat or that activities should be overly structured, but the environment should be functional. The environment communicates a message about the importance you give to physical activity.

Space

Toddlers need an indoor play area to practice physical skills each day. In a home environment, move the furniture around or, if possible, clear out an entire room so you have an open, safe space to move.

In addition to having an indoor space where toddlers can roll balls, toss beanbags into baskets, stack blocks, climb steps, pull toys, and listen to

and move to music, outdoor space also matters. Toddlers need plenty of room for running, jumping, throwing, kicking, and striking. Outdoor space can be found in the backyard, across the street in the yard of a neighbor, or at a local park. This area should be free from safety hazards (such as glass, debris, or water), be located away from buildings or playground structures, and have clearly defined physical boundaries. Remove all obstacles that might hinder a toddler's movement or be a safety concern. Even if you are restricted to a relatively small area, make sure the space is safe by clearing large objects to the corner. Create a safety zone by marking corners of the space with cones or small markers on the ground.

There are no published guidelines for the amount of space appropriate for physical activity at home, but if you want to use standards for school physical-activity settings, NASPE (now called Shape America) recommends at least 150 square feet of open space per child to safely practice skill-development activities. So an open space that is about 10 feet by 15 feet is the minimum space needed for one toddler to practice physical skills.

The term *sedentary* suggests that someone is sitting most of the time and getting very little physical activity. Toddlers are rarely inactive. When they get tired, they may stop activity for a few minutes. Usually, they are soon up and moving again. Sedentary toddlers tend to be those who are in an environment that does not give them opportunities to move. Using the TV as a method of supervising a toddler does not provide him with the physical activity required to develop basic physical skills. Research suggests that, on average, children age two to five spend about thirty-two hours a week in front of a TV. If we really want to reduce childhood obesity and provide an environment that encourages physical activity, we should simply turn off the TV. The American Academy of Pediatrics recommends that children under age two watch no television at all and that children over the age of two watch no more than one to two hours each day.

Skill-Development Equipment

Each part of a child's education requires appropriate learning materials. For example, children learning how to read and write need pencils, crayons, paper, and books. Children learning about math might need pattern blocks, geometric shapes, and counters.

Young children also need appropriate materials and equipment to learn about physical skills. To learn how to throw, a toddler needs different sizes and shapes of balls. To develop skill in striking, toddlers will need a ball and a lightweight racket or plastic bat. When a toddler is developing fine motor skills such as writing, she will need a crayon and paper. When she is learning how to kick, she needs a ball.

In selecting appropriate equipment, be careful to match equipment with the age and skill level of the toddler. For example, a regulation-sized soccer ball would definitely not be suitable for teaching a toddler to kick. Using an adult-sized golf club to teach the toddler striking skills could be disastrous. In each case, the equipment is either too dangerous, too heavy, or simply the wrong size for a toddler trying to develop basic skills.

You may wonder what equipment is needed and where you can find it. Most of what you need to develop basic physical skills can be found in toy or sport retail stores. In general, physical-activity equipment includes balls of different sizes, beanbags, musical instruments, wheeled toys, riding toys, pull and push toys, access to a variety of climbing equipment (local playground or in the backyard), cardboard boxes, tunnels, balance beams, and lightweight striking equipment. Include blocks to stack and other toys to practice fine motor skills. Additional equipment ideas are included throughout the activity section of this book.

Toddlers have a wide range of abilities. They need equipment that challenges them appropriately but will allow them to avoid frustration and have a fun time learning physical skills. The length, size, height, or weight of equipment should be adjusted to meet the toddler's needs. If the ball bounces too high, let some of the air out. If the length of a paddle or bat is too long, find a shorter one.

Equipment Storage

The toddler may not always stop moving long enough to put away his playthings, which can make the activity area look like an obstacle course. Without a storage plan, you will spend time tripping over equipment and looking for lost items that later turn up outside in the rain. The toddler's equipment will need a designated storage spot, but it does not have to be a huge space. It should be the toddler's responsibility to get equipment out and put equipment away. You should take the responsibility of figuring out where equipment should be stored.

A few toddler-friendly strategies will make cleanup easier after play. The following simple ideas will help with equipment storage:

- Decide on a place for storage close to the door, where equipment can be gathered before going outside, or set up storage wherever equipment tends to land. You may have two or three equipment locations.
- It is important that equipment storage be child accessible. Make use of hooks, plastic storage bins or boxes, and open shelves that are sturdy enough for constant use.
- So there is no question about what goes where, label everything. Attach photos to shelves and bins with clear shipping tape.

- Equipment should be easy to get to and move. Consider a small cart with wheels that can be rolled into the backyard or play area. Mesh bags help when transporting several items to the backyard or to the park.

Safety Guidelines

Your goal should be to keep the toddler safe without being overprotective. Equipment for physical activity must be well maintained, and you must provide a safe space without obstacles. This responsibility for the child's safety goes beyond the backyard to any playgrounds or open spaces where you may take the toddler to play. Having a safe environment will help you challenge the toddler to develop physical skills and will help prevent injury, which can turn her off to physical activity. Keep in mind the following basic safety guidelines, whether the play occurs at home or on a playground:

- Check equipment each time you play to make sure nothing is broken. It is a good idea to check when you are gathering equipment to go outside.
- Continually check any playground equipment and the backyard for such dangers as exposed nails and broken parts.

- Do not lift the child onto play equipment that she cannot climb onto by herself. Swings are an exception to this rule, if you can secure the child from falling out.

- Watch out for high places, such as slides and monkey bars, that can be dangerous to young children. Falling from high places is a frequent cause of serious injuries on the playground.

- Allow toddlers to experiment with challenges that build feelings of competence as they are met and mastered, but do not place children at risk.

- You do not need to have a play set in the backyard, but the child should be climbing at least three times each week. If possible, you can go to the local park to climb. Climbing provides the child's large muscles with much-needed exercise and develops strength.

- Supervision—a must with a toddler—is especially critical when the child is on a play structure. Make sure there is always a padded landing surface, such as sand or bark mulch, beneath high equipment, and teach the toddler the best way to land (on both feet with feet wide apart). Grass is not soft enough to adequately cushion a fall.

Creating a toddler-friendly indoor and outdoor physical activity environment takes a bit of planning, but the time and effort will be well worth it. The benefits of having a safe, easy-to-care-for play space will be apparent as you watch the toddler develop physical skills and as you enjoy convenient cleanup and the need for fewer bandages.

MAKE SAFETY A PRIORITY

Safety in the backyard or on the playground should be a top concern for parents and caregivers. A U.S. Consumer Product Safety Commission study found that from 2001 to 2008 more than 200,000 children visited emergency rooms each year for playground-related accidents.

The commission provides a checklist for parents and caregivers to make sure community and school playgrounds are safe places to play:

- Ensure that surfaces around playground equipment consist of least 12 inches of wood chips, mulch, sand, or pea gravel; or use mats made of safety-tested rubber or rubber-like materials.
- Extend protective surfacing at least 6 feet in all directions from the play equipment. For swings, surfacing should extend, in back and front, to twice the height of the suspending bar.
- For play structures more than 30 inches high, make sure they are spaced at least 9 feet apart.
- Check to be sure that the equipment does not have dangerous hardware, such as open *S* hooks or protruding bolt ends.
- Make sure any spaces that could potentially trap children, such as openings in guardrails or between ladder rungs, measure less than 3½ inches or more than 9 inches.
- Check to be sure that equipment does not have sharp points or edges.
- Avoid tripping hazards, such as exposed concrete footings, tree stumps, and rocks.
- Ensure that elevated surfaces, such as platforms and ramps, have guardrails to prevent falls.
- Regularly check to verify that playground equipment and protective surfaces are in good condition.
- Carefully supervise children on playgrounds to keep them safe.

Ideas for Encouraging Physical Activity

Consider the following strategies to help toddlers be active:

- Be a role model and have a positive attitude. If a toddler watches you enjoying physical activity and having fun, it can encourage him to participate.

- Encourage active play, such as going for a fast walk, dancing to music, or riding a tricycle.

- Engage in vigorous activities together such as running; swimming; and playing games that involve kicking, throwing and catching, and striking.

- Encourage family members to be active together—walk with the toddler to a park, ride bikes, or walk the dog.

- Buy gifts that encourage physical activity, such as balls, bats, and push toys.

- Park farther away from your destination—whether it is the school, a sports practice, a sporting event, or a retail shop—so you can walk more.

- Go outside and play every day, rain or shine. Remember how much fun you had as a kid jumping in puddles after it rained?

- Head for the nearest park, use the swing set, or climb on the jungle gym.

Encouraging Physical Activity in Toddlers

Toddler Physical-Activity Playgroups

For home-based care settings, you may want to organize times when children can practice skills with other toddlers. Forming a physical-activity playgroup is a way to get together with children of a similar age and their caregivers. Set a day, time, and place to meet each week in someone's home, in a backyard, or at a local park. Pack some water so everyone remains hydrated during activity.

Children in the playgroup can socialize and make friends while they develop their physical skills. Make sure all toddlers understand the safety rules—you should not need many—so that they do not get too close to each other when swinging a lightweight racket or kicking a ball. Remember, there will be balls flying everywhere! Toddlers will learn by observing each other. If you feel uncomfortable demonstrating certain skills because you cannot do them well, call on other adults in the group to step in. Ideally, start or join a group with three or four toddlers and their caregivers.

You will notice that toddlers do not seem to interact much with each other. At this stage, it is simply not in their nature to play together. A

toddler is usually willing to play alongside another toddler, but asking two toddlers to roll a ball back and forth to each other may not be successful. Organize the toddler group so everyone has equipment, and make sure the adults are in agreement that this is not a time to sit back and relax. All adults will need to supervise the toddlers during group play time just as if the children were playing at home on their own.

Schedule about an hour for the playgroup meetings. Bring a mesh bag full of equipment, and let the toddlers explore and experiment with different equipment items. The playgroup will work best if you select a focus each time you meet. For example, you could work on kicking activities one week and on jumping or throwing activities the next. Have the entire group help put away equipment before going home. It is never too early to introduce children to cooperating with others during physical activity. Getting out and putting away equipment together, throwing balls at the same target, walking together across a log in the woods, or climbing a playground structure with others will help the child develop skills of cooperation. These skills lay the groundwork for positive sportsmanship and enjoyment of cooperative and competitive physical activities in the future.

Encouraging Physical Activity in Toddlers

Plan several activities because toddlers can quickly lose interest with one and be ready to move on to another one. You may need to plan ten to fifteen different physical activities for a one-hour playgroup. For example, have the children play with beanbags while identifying different body parts, throw the beanbags at a target, roll and kick balls, play some music and do some marching, and then get out the musical shakers and march some more. You might take time for a short snack break and a drink before blowing bubbles, doing some running, walking across the balance beam on the playground, and then doing some climbing.

Although you will need lots of activities, keep it simple. Repeat the same activities each week, and add new ones along the way. Also, don't plan your playgroups for more than an hour; the toddlers will be tired. Then it is time for lunch or a nap.

You can get together informally with other caregivers and toddlers or check out local playgroups that are more structured and have an instructor leading the group. A fee may be required to join these groups, but adults searching for information about toddler development may find it valuable to have a knowledgeable instructor. These types of structured groups tend to have more toddlers participating at the same time, and this scenario may not be the best for the toddler in your care.

To help establish the toddler's routine, seek groups that always have a set day and time scheduled for the class and that meet in a regular location.

Search for playgroups in local parenting magazines, at church, at the playground, or at the pediatrician's office. And keep in mind that groups of more than ten toddlers can be overwhelming for the caregivers and the children.

Whether you find a physical-activity group or start your own, remember that successful toddler playgroups start with the right mix of adults who want to make the experience fun.

Tracking Skills

Being able to track an object as it moves through space is an important skill for toddlers to develop if they are to be successful participating in a variety of physical activities. One of the leading reasons children and adults appear uncoordinated in physical activity is because eye-hand (and eye-foot) tracking skills have not been fully developed. Although these skills will improve with age, tracking performance also improves with practice and experience. Some type of tracking activity should be a part of a toddler's daily physical-activity routine.

Development of eye-hand coordination will help toddlers be able to draw and color; catch, kick, and strike balls; and eventually do activities such as putting puzzles together, tying their shoes, using scissors, and threading needles.

Many physical activities, but especially activities with balls, require mature tracking skills to be successful. Although a toddler's vision is fully developed (she can see clearly), toddlers have difficulty tracking moving objects and figuring out how fast they are moving. The process of learning to visually track an object takes time.

Toddlers need lots of practice opportunities to learn to track and to coordinate the movements of their body parts to get in a position to catch or to strike a moving ball. Even an activity such as walking on a balance beam requires the  child's eyes to send a signal to the brain to coordinate picking up the feet to walk across the narrow beam. Physical and visual skills must be coordinated over time, and for most children, this process will not be complete during the toddler years. However, participating in practice activities now will certainly benefit the coordination of tracking and physical skills as the child matures and moves into the preschool years.

TRACKING SKILLS— DID YOU KNOW?

Child-development experts suggest that visual tracking of multiple objects is a critical survival skill. When adults attempt to cross a busy street with cars moving in different directions, they are tracking a number of different objects at the same time. Visual tracking of multiple objects is a complex skill. Imagine the advanced tracking-skill level of a teacher at a child care center attempting to watch twelve toddlers as they play on the playground. The toddler's visual-motor coordination depends on his ability to simultaneously track moving objects.

Encouraging Physical Activity in Toddlers

Eye-Hand Coordination

Eye-hand coordination is the ability of the eyes to guide the hands (or feet) in movement, and it helps toddlers begin to develop physical skills. Eye-hand coordination can help toddlers learn to kick and catch balls and to strike balls with lightweight rackets.

Eye-hand coordination is not just important in learning physical skills; it is also essential in the development of fine motor skills and handwriting and reading. In handwriting, the eyes need to guide the hand in forming letters and making sure the letters are drawn in a straight line across the page. In reading, the eyes must track words in a straight line across the page.

There is no magic formula for helping toddlers develop eye-hand coordination except for daily practice in tracking moving objects. In physical activity and sport settings, many refer to this as "keeping your eyes on the ball."

Tracking Activities

As the toddler works to develop tracking skills, you can participate in fun activities together using flashlights, bubbles, and balls. Some ideas are included here. Set aside ten to fifteen minutes daily to practice this important skill.

Using a Flashlight

One way to work on visual tracking skills with a toddler is to use a flashlight. Any flashlight will work as long as it provides a beam of light to follow. Shine the light on the wall in front of the toddler. Make sure you use a space with no furniture or obstacles to trip over. Move the beam slowly, and ask the toddler to move so he can touch the light on the wall. Move the light up and down and to the right and left. At times move the light fast, and at times move it slowly. Give the flashlight to the toddler, and ask him to move it while you move to touch the beam of light.

Bubbles

The use of bubbles seems to excite toddlers and prompt them to move. In addition to improving tracking skills, bubbles help toddlers develop an understanding of shape, size, and weight. Bubbles are lightweight and float, so they do not behave as balls do. Watching bubbles move through space can help toddlers learn that bubbles rise, fall, move in different directions, and pop.

You can purchase bubble solutions just about anywhere children's toys are sold, or you can make them at home. You may want to experiment with different recipes for homemade bubbles to find which one works best for you and the toddler in your care.

- Mix ¼ cup no-tears baby shampoo, ¾ cup water, and 3 tablespoons light corn syrup.
- Super-strong bubbles can be made with one package unflavored gelatin, 1 cup just-boiled water, 1½ to 2 ounces glycerin (available in the skin-care aisle or at health-food stores), and 8½ ounces baby shampoo. Stir the gelatin into the hot water until it is dissolved. Mix

in the glycerin and shampoo, gently stirring. For extra fun, add food coloring to the mixture. Use the solution right away when it cools enough. If it gets too cool, it will gel, and you will have to reheat it.

- Pour 2 cups of water into a container, and add a half cup of dishwashing liquid. To make bubbles stronger, add 1 tablespoon of glycerin (glycerol), corn syrup, or sugar to the solution.
- Bubble wands can be purchased but are also easy to make at home. Find a small length of wire, and bend one end so it forms a circle for the bubbles. If you want smaller bubbles, form a small circle; larger bubbles require a larger circle. You can bend the other end so that it forms a handle without a sharp end, or use tape to cover the end. Safety note: Make sure no sharp points are exposed so that children do not poke or cut themselves.

Blowing and tracking bubbles with toddlers is really an outside activity (unless it is bath time and parents want to blow the bubbles as their toddler plays in the tub). If you decide to blow bubbles inside, make sure you play on a surface where the toddler will not slip and slide on bubbles that may have reached the floor. Blow bubbles into the air and stand back to watch the action begin. Asking toddlers to reach and touch bubbles is a good way to ease into helping them develop catching skills. You may want to ask them to do some of the following activities.

- Reach to clap hands and pop bubbles (encourages toddlers to get on their tiptoes and stretch many muscles in the body).
- Poke bubbles with a finger.
- Pop bubbles with both left and right hands.
- Jump in the air and strike bubbles with the hands.
- Stomp on bubbles that reach the ground.
- Pop bubbles with different body parts (elbow, fingers, knee, nose, and so on).

Balls

One of the best toys for toddlers is a ball. Balls help the toddler practice skills such as grasping and moving objects from one hand to the other. In addition, balls are excellent for developing tracking skills. For the toddler to have the greatest chances for success, a ball that is at least 8 inches in diameter works best. As children improve their skills, the size of the ball can be reduced, but for young children the larger ball is best. Parents and caregivers should have a variety of different sizes and colors of balls available so the toddler can help choose which ball to use.

No matter what size ball you choose for the toddler to play with, be sure that it can pass the choke-tube test. If the ball can pass through a choke-tube tester, which is about 1 ¼ inches in diameter, then it is too small for the toddler and should not be used.

Beach balls are helpful for tracking activities because they are lighter than most balls and move slowly in the air, giving toddlers time to move their bodies and prepare to catch or strike them. They also work well for partner activities between a toddler and an adult.

You might try the following challenges with beach balls:

- Tap the ball in the air, and ask the toddler to tap it back to you with his hands. To succeed, the toddler will need to watch the beach ball as it travels in the air, move his body under it, and then raise his hands to strike.

- Ask the toddler to strike the beach ball with one hand and then the other, and then with both hands at the same time. Challenge the toddler to hit the ball two times in a row before it hits the floor. As the toddler reaches the age of three, he may be able to continually strike the ball into the air four to six times in a row.

- Practice striking the beach ball with different body parts, including elbows, knees, head, and fists.

- Gently toss the beach ball to the toddler at a low level so he can raise his foot and kick it back to you.

- Tell the toddler to "watch the ball" or "keep your eyes on the ball."
- Beach balls can help a toddler learn directional and space concepts. When you are throwing, catching, or striking balls with the toddler, use concepts in your directions. "Can you strike the ball forward? Can you strike it backward? How about sideways?" "Strike the ball when it is high in the air." "See how high in the air you can make the ball fly."

When you are using other balls that are still appropriate for toddlers, these easy tracking activities can help with eye-hand coordination:

- To develop early ball-handling skills, roll a ball back and forth between you and the toddler. Sit across from each other with your legs spread apart. Using a large, lightweight ball, roll it gently to the toddler, and ask him to try to catch it in his arms and then roll it back to you. As the toddler's skill increases, you can move farther and farther apart. That causes the child to focus on the ball for a longer time and get more practice tracking the ball.
- To add variety to the activity, stand up and roll the ball back and forth, or turn around and roll the ball to the toddler by passing it backward between your legs. If you have a small ramp or slide, roll the ball up and down the ramp.
- Set up a target by turning a large box or empty trash can on its side, and ask the toddler to roll the ball into the target. Or set up two cones—or water bottles, chairs, or anything available that will work—and ask him to roll the ball between the two objects. At first, make sure the objects are far enough apart to promote success. As the toddler improves, move the objects closer together, and ask him to stand farther away and aim the ball between the objects.
- The toddler will love to knock things over. As ball-rolling skills improve, set up some bottle targets, such as empty 16-ounce plastic water bottles set so they are standing up. Ask the toddler to roll the ball and knock down the bottles. You may need to demonstrate the first time, but after that the toddler will lead the way. Keep a box with six to eight empty water bottles available for target practice.

Encouraging Physical Activity in Toddlers

- To further work on tracking skills, explore rolling balls of different sizes and weights down paved ramps and grassy hills. Build ramps out of cardboard tubes, flexible hoses, planks, or PVC pipes, making sure there are no sharp edges that can cut or scrape children! Watch balls as they roll down the ramps. Experiment by using heavier or lighter balls and increasing the steepness of a ramp so the ball moves faster.

In addition to eye-hand and eye-foot activities, encourage the practice and development of fine motor skills. These skills are used daily to complete important tasks such as getting dressed, brushing teeth, feeding oneself, and getting things out and putting them away. Fine motor skills are small, exact movements using the thumb, finger, hand, and wrist to manipulate objects. Try some of the following activities to help develop and improve these important skills.

- Drawing and scribbling start sometime between twelve and eighteen months of age. By twenty-four months, many toddlers will begin to draw horizontal and vertical lines, and some may start to draw circles. Children will have fun scribbling on large sheets of paper taped to a table. Use thick, oversized crayons for a toddler's initial attempts at drawing. Use chalk for sidewalk drawing, set up an easel for brush painting, or tape paper onto a patio table outside for fingerpainting.

- Let children fill up containers and dump them out. These motions require some precise practice using the thumb and forefinger. Before snack time, have the toddler wash his hands. Place a cup of raisins on the table, and ask him to dump them out on a napkin. Then ask him to fill up the cup one raisin at a time. Afterward, the child has a snack at his fingertips!

- Provide sorting activities using different-shaped wooden blocks so the toddler can place all the squares and triangles together.

- An older toddler will have the skill to string doughnut-shaped cereal (such as Cheerios) onto a clean shoestring. Wash hands first, of course! Have the child take the cereal pieces off one by one for a snack afterward.

Encouraging Physical Activity in Toddlers

- Practice balancing blocks on top of one another to construct a tower. Knock down the tower and start again.
- Putting clothes on and taking them off can initially be challenging for toddlers. Provide pants with elastic waists and shoes with Velcro. Put together a box of dress-up clothes, including items with large buttons and snaps to give older toddlers some practice manipulating these fasteners.
- Felt boards are great for giving children a surface on which they can pick up felt animal shapes and move them around.

- Encourage the toddler to help you in the kitchen. Stirring, measuring, and tasting are all great fine motor practice. Find a toddler-sized rolling pin, so he can roll out cookie dough. Use cookie cutters to make shapes out of healthy sandwiches. You can also let him toss salad with two large spoons.
- Take the toddler to the beach or park where he can sit with his bucket, fill it full of sand, and make sand castles.

Strength
Development

4

Development of most physical skills depends on a toddler having strong muscles. Muscular strength gives children the ability to apply force and effort to move. Large muscles develop before small muscles—for example, the muscles used to control a toddler's neck, back, arms, and legs develop before the muscles in her fingers and hands. Toddlers learn gross motor skills, such as running, jumping, and kicking, before they learn fine motor skills, such as drawing or tying shoes.

Do not worry about doing a lot of specific strength activities to build toddlers' muscles; just being physically active each day will go a long way toward helping toddlers gain strength. They will naturally spend most of the day working their muscles by climbing, traveling, balancing, jumping, throwing, catching, and kicking. The more a toddler uses her muscles during daily activity, the stronger she will become.

Climbing

Toddlers love to climb. Climbing is a natural part of healthy physical development, and as soon as the toddler begins to walk he will also show interest in climbing to a higher level. He has finally developed the muscular strength to pull up and will take every opportunity he can to look at his environment from a different, higher point of view.

Climbing is considered a locomotor or traveling skill and is an important physical milestone for toddlers. Toddlers climb everywhere—they will try to climb on chairs, up on the kitchen table, or onto a desk or cabinet—so supervision is very important to their safety. Be sure to instruct the toddler not to climb on inappropriate or dangerous structures, and be there to support or catch the child—called *spotting*—when needed. Climbing helps the toddler see the world from a different level and develop muscular strength in the arms, legs, and hands. Hand strength, in particular, is important to fine motor control and learning how to write.

Overall muscular strength helps the child learn new skills such as walking up and down stairs, kicking a ball, and balancing without falling over or running into objects.

Climbing is one of those physical activities that children naturally attempt. You don't have to teach this skill; you just let it happen and supervise. Any playground structure will seem to naturally inspire the toddler to want to climb. Climbing gives the toddler the opportunity to exercise the vestibular system and develop balance and strength. Pulling up with the hands and arms while climbing a child-size ladder or a playground structure builds upper-body, grip, and arm strength, and climbing steps and ladders develops leg strength and coordination. Of course, you will need to limit where and how high toddlers climb.

BUILDING STRENGTH—DID YOU KNOW?

Climbing trees and playground structures used to be standard practice for most children. During the past ten years, there has been a shift away from outdoor physical activities and an increase in the use of computers by children. Children are becoming weaker, demonstrating less muscular strength, and finding themselves unable to do the physical tasks that youngsters did in previous generations. Research suggests that children are becoming more unfit, less active, and more sedentary; in many cases, they are heavier than children in previous decades. Toddlers are not typically evaluated for strength, but research has found that both arm strength and grip strength have declined in elementary-age children. *The Guardian* newspaper highlighted a study finding that ten-year-olds in 2008 could do fewer sit-ups and were less able to climb and hang from bars on the playground than children that age in 1998. With toddlers, you can promote healthy physical activity by finding opportunities for them to climb safely and participate in other strength activities as often as possible. That way, when they get older and climb trees, they will have the strength and experience to handle it safely.

Climbing helps teach the muscles and the brain to work together and helps the child coordinate movements on both sides of the body. As a toddler climbs, the brain tells the left hand and right foot to move together and then tells the right hand and left foot to move together. His eyes work with his brain to focus on where to grab and hold on and where to place his feet.

When a toddler climbs, he not only develops eye-hand coordination and balance but also learns about consequences. Yes, the toddler is going to have some falls while learning to climb, but he will quickly understand his capabilities and become more cautious.

A toddler is going to climb whether you want him to or not. You can provide practice and support by making climbing part of the daily routine and ensuring a safe environment for these activities.

- Provide safe places and equipment for the toddler to get experience climbing. Let him climb on indoor and outdoor play gyms, and provide a sturdy children's step stool so he can climb to reach toys or books on a table or shelf.

- Anticipate accidents. Climb-proof the home or child-care space. Place any wobbly or unstable furniture (chairs, small tables, bookcases) in a room away from where the child will play, or pack furniture away in the garage until he is older. Make sure bookcases are securely attached to the wall, and do not leave stools or stepladders out where the toddler can climb when you are not looking. Keep chairs pushed under the table.

- Set up gates at the top and bottom of stairs until the toddler can climb up and down without needing assistance.

- This will be a new phrase for some, but you are now on *catch duty*. Whenever the toddler is climbing, be there to catch him in case he falls.

Encouraging Physical Activity in Toddlers

- Another way to encourage a younger toddler to climb is to provide some mats or small boxes to climb over. Initially, items to climb over do not have to be large. Place a sofa cushion on the floor and watch as the toddler moves to climb over the cushion.

Climbing Furniture

Although climbing on furniture may be fun and challenging for the toddler, it is not always safe. The toddler will become very enthusiastic about climbing and will attempt to do so frequently. Don't yell at or scold him for doing something that is a natural part of growing up, but do set limits, such as not climbing on furniture or cabinets. You can redirect him to safer and more appropriate climbing activities and make them part of the daily routine.

Climbing Stairs

For many children, climbing actually begins before walking. Most children will attempt to climb stairs in home-based care by using hands and feet to crawl up and slide down. Increase your supervision when children begin climbing, and make sure you are there to catch them if they fall off balance. Most will start climbing before they can do so safely. Children will attempt to pull themselves up onto a step, and then another, and then another. At that point, the child may be stuck and not able to safely get back down to the bottom of the steps. Demonstrate how the child can lie on his belly and slowly slide down feet first. What goes up will always come down!

Watch closely, as toddlers will sneak away just to attempt the challenge of climbing stairs. Sit right next to the child on the stairs to help prevent falls, and watch as he maneuvers his body to go up and down the steps. Don't help the young toddler; let him figure it out. Most toddlers will not master stair climbing until about thirty-six months of age.

Most toddlers will demonstrate the ability to walk up stairs by themselves before they are able to walk down stairs unassisted. Walking up and down stairs will appear uncoordinated for several months because the height of a stair was constructed for an adult—not a toddler's shorter legs. If a child is not making progress on walking up and down steps by age three, parents should discuss concerns with the child's pediatrician.

When the toddler begins walking up and down stairs, you need to be there with a hand to hold onto and let him use the rail for support. By about twenty-four months of age, most toddlers have begun the process of learning how to walk up and down stairs by themselves. Most will need initial assistance holding an adult's hand or the handrail for support.

The next challenge for the toddler will be to climb a short ladder or climb up an outdoor playground structure. Never allow the toddler to climb when a playground structure is wet. Emphasize that the toddler needs to move slowly when climbing a ladder and to hold on tight when gripping the rungs.

Being able to climb on playground structures is an important physical milestone for toddlers. Climbing equipment should not be higher than 3 feet off the ground for children this age. Here are some ideas and ways to help.

- Start with short, easy climbs. Don't lift or push; just be there to provide a hand when needed.
- Guide the child to grasp the bars or structure tightly, and move his feet slowly.
- Climbing down is as important as climbing up. Advise the child to grasp tightly and move slowly. Don't allow him to jump down from a high level; ask him to climb all the way down until his feet are on the ground.
- Talk with the toddler while he is climbing. Tell him where he might place his hands or feet if he looks like he needs help.
- Tell the child to keep his hands higher than his feet and find safe holds to grab onto. If he can't figure out where to hold on, point out some good spots.
- When a toddler is climbing a ladder on the playground, show him how to grasp tightly and hold onto the rungs of the ladder when climbing up, going up one step at a time. Also work with the toddler to help him learn how to climb down, stepping down with one foot at a time and sliding his hands slowly down the ladder.

Some toddlers may seem frustrated and ask for help in the beginning, so look for small successes.

Playgrounds and parks provide a variety of different types of equipment for climbing, but supervision of the child during the toddler years will be more important and time-consuming than during any other time. Understand that when the toddler is experimenting with climbing, he will fall, and you will need to be within arm's reach ready to catch.

Make sure the ground around the outdoor equipment provides a soft landing. Do not allow the toddler to climb equipment that is above a hard, paved, or concrete surface.

When the child begins climbing, a few minutes is plenty.

If the toddler is not interested or is scared to climb on the playground, do not force him. He will tell you when he is ready. If the child is timid about heights, let him hang around at the bottom of the playground structure. Eventually he will begin to watch others climb and will want to do it himself. Children with older brothers and sisters may be more willing to take on a playground structure. You can't really stop a climber, and safe climbing helps children build strength and balance. It also is an excellent way for children to gain confidence in their physical skills.

Hanging

Hanging refers to the toddler holding onto an object above the head with the hands. Hanging activities help strengthen the muscles in the arms and shoulders and build strength to encourage climbing. Activities could be as simple as the toddler holding onto your hands or a stick as you lift her off the ground. The child can also hold onto a bar on a playground structure.

Hanging from a stick is a good beginning activity. Stand facing the toddler, and hold onto a 1-foot-long dowel stick with both hands. As an alternative, you can use a broom handle. Ask the child to grasp the stick in both hands, then place your hands on top of hers to prevent her grip from slipping. Lift her about 4 inches off the ground, and let her hang for a count of five before lowering her to the ground. Increase the amount of time she hangs in the air. As the toddler learns to grasp the stick on her

own, you will no longer need to provide support by holding her hands. For young toddlers, four or five lifts each day will help develop strength. You will not be able to continue this activity with an older toddler, as she may be too heavy to lift. Then the child can hang from a bar on a playground structure.

Older toddlers will think they can practice hanging on the playground without adult assistance, but they still need your help. Find a playground structure with a bar that allows the toddler to hang with her feet no more than 6 inches off the ground. If you lift a toddler to hold onto a bar that is higher, you will need to place your hands around the child's hips so you are ready to catch her when she lets go. In the beginning, let the toddler hang for ten to twenty seconds, and then lower her to the ground. By the time the child is three, she will be able to grasp and hold without letting go for sixty to ninety seconds. Many three-year-olds will be able to hold on for several minutes.

Music
and
Physical
Activity

Have you ever watched what happens to toddlers when music is playing? They move! Music and physical activity naturally go together. Research suggests that children who are actively involved in music (who play it, sing it, or listen to it regularly) do better in reading and math when they start school, are better able to focus and control their bodies, and play better with others. Moving to music helps young children learn about their body parts and understand how to move to a rhythmical pattern. This understanding may help the child know when to swing a bat to strike a ball, coordinate when to swing the leg forward to kick, or synchronize how to move body parts smoothly when galloping or skipping. Music helps toddlers develop a sense of patterning during movement activities.

Introduce music by playing it in the background while you and the toddler sing songs, clap your hands, and dance. Music helps the toddler learn about rhythm and timing and develop physical coordination. By moving and dancing to music and playing simple instruments, toddlers will improve their gross and fine motor skills. Also, swaying back and forth and shifting weight from one foot to the other helps improve their balance.

Music is important to a toddler's overall growth and development for many reasons. Teachers and researchers agree that music can help develop children's language skills, self-esteem, listening skills, and math skills, and it encourages creativity. Some experts assert that music can serve as a fundamental skill of learning and is as important as learning the alphabet, numbers, or how to kick or throw a ball.

Just about any type of music can stir the toddler to movement. Children respond well to songs with a repeating rhythm and a cheerful beat. You might have less success using loud rap or rock music that does not have a consistent rhythm. When children need to rest after physical activity, soothing tunes work well; music can help calm toddlers and relieve stress. To make the transition to nap time, try playing soft tunes to help toddlers fall asleep.

Moving with Rhythm

Experiences involving rhythm support physical development and can help young children as they learn to run, gallop, jump, and increase fine motor coordination. Musical activities also help children develop the rhythm and timing needed to be able to throw, catch, and strike a ball. Provide toddlers with music and movement activities each day to help them learn to enjoy music and to assist with motor-skill development. Consider the following ideas as you incorporate music:

- Select all types of music to listen to—including songs with a slow tempo and a fast beat. The music doesn't have to be designed for toddlers; you can also try classical and jazz, for example.

RHYTHMIC INSTRUMENTS

As soon as infants can grasp and hold objects, they will begin to shake and bang things on the floor. Toddlers continue these activities as a way to explore their environment and experiment with creating sounds. Rhythm instruments are easy to use and will stimulate the toddler to explore different ways to move.

If you would like to incorporate an instrument while you are moving to music, keep it simple. Younger toddlers will enjoy instruments they can shake—bells, rattles, shakers, tambourines, and rhythm sticks. Older toddlers who have become more coordinated are ready for rhythm instruments that can be tapped or struck, such as drums, cymbals, or xylophones.

You can create hundreds of fun, appropriate musical activities for toddlers using instruments such as maracas, tambourines, rhythm sticks, drums, and bells. Just about anything that makes a noise can help a toddler learn rhythm and timing and develop a love for music.

- Turn on music in the background instead of TV as you go through the day's activities, including play time.
- Have scheduled times during the day that you move and dance to music.
- Help toddlers recognize rhythmical patterns and identify musical beats. Join children in marching activities. Show them how to stomp their feet, clap their hands, and strike or tap drums and other objects with wooden spoons or rhythm sticks.
- Provide toys that allow toddlers to create their own music.

As you plan your daily routine, include moving to music, listening to tunes, singing, and playing instruments. By listening, a toddler begins to understand the difference between soft and loud compositions and to recognize changes in rhythm. Singing helps him form listening and language skills; it can also help with rhythm as he moves to the beat and sings along. Experimenting with sounds while playing instruments also contributes to his development of rhythm.

A sense of rhythm and timing will help the toddler as he begins learning to throw, catch, and strike a ball; each of these skills is considered a timed motor task. The child will need to understand timing to know when to place his arms out in front of his body to catch a ball or when to swing a bat to strike accurately. The development of a sense of rhythm and timing is essential to success in physical activity.

The *beat* in music is the recurring rhythmic pulse that is heard or felt throughout the song. You can design activities that will help toddlers synchronize their movements to the beat. Have them bang on drums, walk, run, or gallop to the beat of the music. Do not become frustrated if the toddler does not get the hang of it immediately. By age three, most children are able to move to the beat of music.

Repetition of music activities is the key to learning about music and to developing physical skills. Young children love to repeat things. Listening to the same music over and over encourages the use of words and memorization. Repeating movements to music helps a toddler develop movement patterns that will improve physical skills. Playing a toddler's favorite song over and over helps him learn.

Stages of Understanding

As in all areas of early learning, a toddler will progress through stages in her musical development. In general, toddlers can learn short, simple songs and will attempt to sing along with the words, although they can rarely carry a tune. Even though a toddler will sing songs and repeat the words over and over, she will seldom sing with a group. A toddler usually can follow directions in songs and will have several favorites that she asks you to play over and over. Toddlers tend to enjoy experimenting with the different sounds they can make by shaking musical instruments, beating on pots and pans, and clapping their hands. They also should be able to understand that the tempo of music can be fast or slow.

Developmentally, toddlers should be exposed to music and movement activities where they can:

- Move their bodies in response to different types of music;
- Learn short, simple songs;
- Follow the directions in songs;
- Move their bodies and body parts to specific musical beats and keep a beat with a variety of musical instruments;
- Experiment with sounds and movement (march to the beat of a drum or clap their hands while marching); and
- Run, gallop, or jump to music.

Listening to and moving to music can promote the development of several important toddler skills:

- Gross and fine motor skills, body awareness, coordination, and timing
- Learning concepts such as levels, pathways, directions, speeds (fast and slow beats), and sounds (loud and soft)
- Thinking skills such as staying on task, problem solving, following instructions, and increasing attention span
- Language skills such as learning new words and their meanings, following patterns, and counting

Don't expect toddlers to be able to sing in tune or have much rhythmic ability; remember, they are just getting started learning about music. The movement and music activities you do will lay a foundation for development of musical and physical skills as they advance through the preschool years.

Interlimb Coordination

Using music with movement will help develop what is called *interlimb coordination,* which makes a toddler's hands and feet work together and is linked with his ability to learn many basic motor skills. Interlimb coordination involves the ability to use both sides of the body together so motor skills flow naturally. Being able to swing both arms forward when jumping forward is an example of interlimb coordination. If both arms do not swing forward at the same time, the jump will appear awkward and the toddler may not be able to land on balance.

Simple skills such as clapping hands or jumping and landing on two feet require the hands and feet on different sides of the body to work together to accurately perform the skill. More complex skills—such as galloping and skipping, or placing one foot on the ground beside a ball and kicking the ball with the other foot—require a higher level of coordination of body parts to perform well.

Children who do not develop interlimb coordination can appear uncoordinated when they walk because their arms do not swing in opposition. They also tend to have difficulty throwing because they cannot coordinate the proper placement of their arms and legs. Most basic motor skills require some level of interlimb coordination. Toddlers need opportunities to practice using their body parts so they can synchronize or rhythmically time movements of the arms and legs.

The following activities involve interlimb coordination, and many of them can be practiced with music played at different rhythmic beats. Try having the toddler do the following:

- Tap his fingers, hands, or sticks to rhythmic beats
- Draw circles with both hands at the same time
- Clap his hands in time to a musical beat
- Do a variety of fingerplay songs such as "Itsy Bitsy Spider" or clapping games that require the hands and fingers to work together
- Alternate opening and closing of the hands
- Imitate animals that move forward, backward, and sideways
- Catch a ball with two hands
- Gallop and then try alternating the foot that leads

For an older toddler, you can place two small balls on the floor in front of the child and two small shoe boxes next to the balls. Ask him to pick up both balls, one in each hand, at the same time and then drop them in the boxes.

By age three, a child should be able to march to the beat of a song, continuing through to the end. Initially, clapping hands to the beat is easier for toddlers than clapping hands to the beat while also walking or marching. But with practice, they will get the hang of marching and clapping.

When the toddler learns to clap, structures in the brain are working to connect the two sides of the brain and help them communicate. As the toddler's brain develops, he will become better at performing actions that require both sides of the body to move in a coordinated way. Playing clapping games at an early age can help strengthen this development, leading to strong connections between both sides of the brain. At around age four, most children have developed the ability to fully control and synchronize the movements of both hands. Children need practice to coordinate physical skills that require the right arm and hand to work with those on the left, and the left leg and foot to work with those on the right.

Add clapping to the toddler's daily physical activities because clapping games improve the toddler's fine motor skills and eye-hand coordination. Most infants have the ability to clap their hands together sometime between nine and twelve months of age. You may start with traditional clapping activities such as patty-cake or clapping at appropriate points in the song "If You're Happy and You Know It." But don't stop with these simple songs—any music with a rhythmic beat can be a good clap-along song.

Scarves

Scarves are lightweight and lots of fun for toddler movement activities. They can help children learn about pathways and levels in space. Moving the scarf in different pathways, such as circles, zigzag, and straight, and at high and low levels·around the body will help the toddler begin to understand these scientific concepts as well as reinforce other concepts such as up, down, and sideways directions, and fast and slow pace. Give the toddler a scarf, and watch the activity begin. When she runs out of ideas, you can suggest more to encourage additional movement.

If you don't want to buy a scarf, you can make one by cutting a square out of lightweight material. For toddlers, the ideal size of the scarf is a square that measures 10 inches to 16 inches on one side. Larger scarves may not be appropriate, as the toddler may step on the edge of the scarf and trip. If you make your own scarves, make sure you get lightweight material that gently floats through the air. A large paper towel can be used as an inexpensive alternative. Model how to hold the scarf by a corner when moving it around your body. By doing so, the toddler will be able to see the pathway the scarf makes as it moves through the air.

To get started, make sure the toddler has a scarf in her hand, then turn on some music and model different ways the scarf might move. Swish the scarf around your body in front and to the side, then high in the air and low to the ground. Move fast and slow to the beat of the music. Now have the toddler try the following activities, as you continue to model the movements when needed:

- Move freely around the movement space holding the scarf out and letting it flow through the air
- Make figure eights in the air with the scarf

Encouraging Physical Activity in Toddlers

- Turn, twist, twirl, and spin in circles
- Switch hands, holding the scarf in one hand and then in the other
- Jump and leap in the air while moving the scarf in different pathways
- Move the scarf in front of the body in a pattern similar to windshield wipers on a car
- Hang the scarf down, and move it back and forth as if sweeping the floor
- Move the scarf in big circles in front, to the side, and overhead
- Walk around and wave the scarf in the air like a flag

With older toddlers, you can also play follow the leader, asking the toddler to follow you and do what you do with the scarf. Then ask the child to be the leader, and you follow her actions.

Ribbons and Streamers

Purchase ribbon that is 1½ to 2 inches wide, and cut the length to about 4 feet. You can cut longer lengths for older children, but a ribbon or streamer that is too long is likely to get tangled around a toddler's body. In fact, a shorter length may be needed for a toddler's initial play. Streamers with handles or sticks to hold onto can also be purchased. Streamers made of crepe paper work well too. Purchase a roll of 2-inch-wide crepe paper at a local party store, and cut it into lengths. (You might want to get a big roll, as toddlers enjoy doing this activity with friends!) As the child gets older and can better control the streamer, you can increase the length.

To begin, turn on some music, ask the toddler to hold the end of the ribbon, and let the fun begin! Encourage him to dance and move the ribbon freely, watching the pathways in which the ribbon moves.

Suggest that he move the streamer fast, slowly, low, high, side to side, and in curved, zigzag, and circular pathways. Ask the toddler to move the ribbon like the wipers on the car, circle the streamer in the front of his body, sweep the floor with the streamer, and place the ribbon on the floor and move it like a snake. At this initial stage of rhythm development, most toddlers will not be able to move the ribbon to the beat of any music. The idea is to explore how to move the ribbons in space and have fun moving to music.

Rhythm-Stick Activities

Rhythm sticks are musical instruments that make sounds when you tap them together. They can be purchased in toy stores or through music catalogs, or you can make your own.

Rhythm sticks are a natural extension of toddlers clapping their hands and stomping their feet. The sticks help the toddler continue to coordinate his ability to time movements and develop movement patterns. Using rhythm sticks is a process, though, and it will take some time before the toddler is actually striking the sticks together at the appropriate time with the music. Play with the rhythm sticks several times each week, repeating activities over and over. All this repetition will increase her coordination and timing.

Playing with rhythm sticks helps toddlers with fine motor development because they have to use the small muscles of their hands and fingers to hold the sticks and strike them together. The sticks also promote eye-hand coordination and eye tracking as the child follows the sticks while they are moving. Stick activities help a toddler coordinate moving body parts smoothly. Playing with the sticks also fosters listening skills as she strives to hear and identify different sounds.

It works best if you practice movements together using the rhythm sticks before the child attempts to tap in time to the music. Select music with a rhythmic beat that is slow enough for the toddler to follow successfully, and then have a great time making music.

Marching

Give the toddler a stick for each hand, play some good marching music, and then go off together to march in a parade. Ask the child to follow as you march around the room striking sticks together. Then it is the toddler's turn to lead, and you follow.

Tapping Activities

You can do this activity sitting down facing each other, but the toddler will still be moving his arms. If several children are playing, make sure everyone has enough space to safely use their sticks. The first few times you try the tapping activities, you should model movements for the toddlers and provide any verbal instruction needed.

- "Can you use your sticks like drumsticks and pretend to play the drum?" The toddler should strike the sticks on the floor as if playing the drums.
- "Can you play the drum softly?" "Can you play the drum loudly?"
- "Let's put the drum beat and striking sticks together in a pattern. Can you strike the sticks down on the floor and then strike them together?"

"Down, together, down, together, down, together." "Strike the sticks first down on the floor to your side then together in front of you."

- "Let's pretend to build a house, using one stick for the nail and the other stick for the hammer. Hold the nail straight up with one end on the floor and strike the other end with your hammer. Be careful not to hit your hand with the hammer."

- "We have been working so hard, and I am getting hungry. Let's pretend to peel a carrot for lunch." Model the action by holding the sticks, one in each hand, and scraping them together as if peeling a carrot.

- Ask the toddler to hold the sticks above his head and strike the sticks together.

Traveling Skills

CHAPTER

6

Traveling or locomotor skills—including walking, running, climbing, and galloping—help children move from one place to another and are the most basic in a toddler's foundation of physical skills. Before walking, his only traveling skills were to scoot, roll, and crawl. Now that he can stand and walk, exploration of his world becomes easier.

A toddler will accomplish many physical milestones related to development of traveling skills. By the time he is three, he will be able to gallop and will enjoy climbing, walking up and sliding down inclines, walking forward and backward while changing directions and speeds, walking up and down stairs, and running. Skipping is also a traveling skill, but the child will be into the preschool years before skipping skills emerge.

Unlike many of the other basic skills that need adult guidance and instruction to learn, traveling skills come naturally to most children. The best approach to introducing these skills to toddlers is to model them and perform the movements alongside the children. When needed, provide modeling instructions such as "Watch how I swing my arms when I walk," or "See how I keep one foot in front when galloping." Toddlers need lots of time to practice traveling skills so these skills can naturally develop.

Moving by traveling does not require any special equipment, and it is one of the best ways to get a child's heart moving faster and to expend energy. Practice traveling skills for a few minutes each time you take children outside to play. "Let's gallop to the mailbox," or "Let's run to the tree and back."

Walking

Infants begin the process of learning to walk by pulling themselves to a standing position and holding onto furniture. When standing, a toddler will strengthen her muscles and begin taking small steps. She will learn to stand without support, bend her knees to squat, and take steps while holding onto a caregiver's hands. When tired, she will learn to lower herself into a squatting position and then will sit down. The child will begin walking with her feet turned outward and initially will spend most of her time walking on her tiptoes.

Walking involves lifting and setting down each foot while moving forward but never having both feet off the ground at the same time. Now that the toddler can stand, walking becomes the favorite way to move through the environment. The mature walking pattern is smooth with straight steps and with arms swinging in opposition to the feet. Her head should be up so she can see where she is moving. When she stops, she should stay on balance without falling over.

Most toddlers move through a predictable sequence in learning how to walk. You may notice that after a few months of walking, the toddler will demonstrate a longer step and then will begin to hold her arms at the sides instead of out in front. When the toddler begins to run, she will use her arms in opposition to her legs, with the elbows bent and the arms swinging. At some point, she will move from walking on her tiptoes to placing her heel on the ground first and then pushing off with her toes.

A toddler's walk may appear awkward, off balance, and jerky early on, but by age three most children have developed the walking skills needed to efficiently move through daily activities. Do not be alarmed when a toddler falls; this is part of the process of learning to walk. Initially, you may want to have the child explore walking on carpeted surfaces and away from furniture. After a few months, she will have developed the strength and balance to be able to pull toys and pick up and carry objects while walking. Between two and three years of age, she will become confident enough in walking that she can walk to kick a ball.

You can help by setting up an environment that promotes development of a mature walking pattern. Provide an obstacle-free area to practice, making sure there are no toys or other items to trip over or fall on. As the toddler gets older and demonstrates the ability to stay on balance when walking, provide some small obstacles to step over, such as a rope or a hoop on the floor. This will encourage her to lift her feet higher off the floor and will help strengthen leg musclesin preparation for standing on one foot and for marching. Obstacles should not be more than 6 inches high, depending on her ability to balancewhen stepping over items. Place several obstacles on the floor in a row, and ask the toddler to walk in a line and step over each of them. You will create the toddler's first obstacle course!

A toddler's clothing and shoes should not restrict movement. Actually, some podiatrists recommend that toddlers not wear shoes often when learning to walk. As much as possible, they say, you should allow the child to learn to walk in bare feet, wearing shoes only when needed to protect from environmental dangers. If you live in a cold climate, you can provide socks that are nonskid for indoor practice. When the child is walking outside, select shoes that are flexible and lightweight, and avoid the type that provide a lot of ankle support.

You might consider getting the toddler a push toy, which provides a place for her to grip. A push toy gives the toddler control and balance as she pushes it forward; the pushing can also help strengthen the leg muscles.

Make sure your schedule includes rest times during the day. The toddler will get tired and may demonstrate some frustration while walking around. Some toddlers may cling to you—especially late in the day— and want to be picked up and carried. Remember that walking is hard work for toddlers, and they need frequent rest periods.

A word of warning—do not put the toddler in a walker! Walkers can tip over and be a safety hazard. Furthermore, research suggests that a walker can slow motor development and cause back problems. Toddlers need to develop muscular strength to walk, and a walker restricts movement.

Marching

Just about anytime music is playing, a toddler will want to get up and start moving. Marching is a good way for children to develop balance and

Encouraging Physical Activity in Toddlers

coordination. When toddlers march, they use an exaggerated walking step. They raise their knees as high as possible on each step, and their arms, with elbows bent, swing in opposition. Marching is excellent preparation for eventually being able to stand on one foot. The movement also helps the child develop a sense of rhythm.

Practice marching to music daily. It's even more fun when you invite other toddlers and caregivers to march with you! Consider the following ideas, as well as the other music and movement activities in Chapter 5.

● Start by demonstrating how the toddler should raise his knees high as he walks; this movement becomes marching.

● Play upbeat music. Move to the beat of the music, emphasizing raising the knees high in the air each time he takes a step.

● March while clapping hands or tapping two sticks together. Use a drum or shake a rhythm instrument as you and the toddler march to the beat.

- Move at different speeds; beat on a drum or strike sticks slowly or quickly to set the marching rhythm.
- Play some marching music and start a parade. Music with a consistent rhythmic beat is great for marching.
- Play follow the leader, and ask the toddler to copy your marching pattern. Then ask him to be the marching leader.

Galloping

Galloping is included here because some toddlers will begin developing this skill at about thirty months of age. Others, however, may not demonstrate it until age three or four. Galloping is an exaggerated slide step composed of a step and a leap. The front leg is lifted and bent, then thrust forward to support the weight of the toddler. The rear foot quickly closes to replace the supporting leg as the front leg springs forward again. Children typically learn to gallop before they learn to hop or skip. Although learning to gallop may appear to be easy, it does take some practice to master.

When you introduce galloping, ask the toddler to take a big step forward, keeping that foot in front of the body at all times. The child should start moving forward by stepping on the front foot and then bringing the rear foot forward. When toddlers learn to gallop, challenge them to gallop everywhere. "Gallop to the tree and back." "Let's gallop together over to the playground equipment and back." Set up some cones in a grassy area, and gallop in circles around the obstacles. When galloping with toddlers, always gallop on a level surface so no one trips and falls. Make sure you are several feet away from the child so there is always enough room to gallop together without bumping into each other.

Running

Running is the basis of most sport activities, but adults should understand that learning to run is not a sport. The initial steps in learning to run are all about keeping your balance, learning that the arms swing when running, and moving the body faster than it has moved before. Learning to run is not about running races or trying to beat a fellow toddler across the playground; it is all about having fun while experimenting with what the body can do.

Initially, running will take a lot of concentration, as the toddler will be able to run only in a straight line for short distances and at a slow speed. Somewhere around two years of age, the toddler will be able to run around things that are in her path and increase her speed without falling. Learning to run is not about warming up or stretching out—the toddler's muscles do not need to be stretched. Running as a toddler is all about moving the feet forward, faster and faster, and swinging the arms in opposition.

Most toddlers love to run and use what seems to be endless energy. The best way to introduce this skill is to take her outside and run together. She is not going to go for extended distances at first. To a younger toddler, running fast for 15 to 20 feet is like running 100 yards is to an adult. When you go play in the park, in the backyard, or on the playground, encourage the toddler to run back and forth between two adults. Provide

As skill in running develops and toddlers begin to enjoy chasing games, make sure they understand that they are not to run away when you call. This is a difficult concept for most toddlers to grasp, but it is a safety issue. You do not want the toddler to run from you if she is in a dangerous situation, so start educating her to come to you when you request it. Make sure she understands that running is acceptable when playing a game but running away is not when you ask her to stay close or come to you.

a big hug and then send her back to the other adult for another hug. You can also encourage her by challenging her to run like her favorite animal. "Can you run like a lion?" Another fun activity is to blow bubbles into the air and ask the toddler to chase and pop them. Playing chase with the toddler is a great way to encourage running practice. Run until the toddler wants to stop. Stop and rest a few minutes, then run some more.

Encouraging Physical Activity in Toddlers

You may notice that some toddlers have an efficient, smooth running pattern and others run flat-footed with their heads moving from side to side and arms swinging all over the place. When a toddler demonstrates an efficient pattern, you will see arm and leg opposition, the toes pointing forward, the arms bent at the elbow and swinging next to the body, and the upper body leaning forward slightly. It takes several years for children to develop this pattern. The best way to help toddlers learn to run better is to ask them to run fast. Running at a fast pace requires a child to use the arms and legs in opposition and to swing the arms to be efficient.

Developing Balance

Toddlers have already developed a lot of skill in balancing to be able to stand up and begin walking, but they need to continue developing balance so they can climb, run, gallop, throw, and kick. They need this skill to move safely and participate in daily activities. Balance will help them climb ladders, walk on logs, land without falling when they jump, and stay upright when they kick balls. Each day, a toddler's physical activities will involve balance, so he is actually practicing just about every time he moves.

Balance may be the most important skill the toddler can develop because it is a required part of performing all other skills. Balance is required as the infant learns to crawl, sit, and stand, and as the four-year-old jumps to take off in flight and lands without falling over. It also is important to the toddler's safety: Young children develop balance so they can walk without falling, ride a tricycle without tumbling over, or kick a ball without falling on their bottoms. Balance gets better with practice and is an important foundation for successful participation in all types of physical activity, including future sports.

Balance skills are task specific, which means that a toddler may do very well in one balance activity and not as well in another. Age is also a significant factor in performance of balance activities. As a toddler gets older, balance skills will improve in relation to growth and strengthening of the child's muscles and bones. Success in balance depends largely on age, experience, and practice.

Vestibular System

A toddler's sense of balance hinges on connections in the vestibular sensory system in the inner ear. Swinging, jumping, spinning, rocking, and climbing are fun, but they also help the body organize and regulate the vestibular system. This system responds to movement and gravity, contributing to the development of balance, posture control, and maintaining a stable visual field while moving. Being physically active throughout life depends partly on development of the vestibular system and practicing and improving balance skills.

The toddler's vestibular system is really a feedback loop among the eyes, brain, and inner ear and needs stimulation to function correctly. The toddler's brain will register all the twists and turns of her body and will send signals to the muscles on what to do to maintain balance. Any type of activity that places the toddler in an off-balance position so that she has to move to stay on balance will strengthen the vestibular system.

Activities such as bouncing, rocking, and swinging force the inner ear to send messages to the brain, and then the brain sends messages to the muscles so that the toddler can remain upright and not feel dizzy. The vestibular system helps the toddler walk without falling over or move through a room full of obstacles without bumping into a chair or table.

SWINGING— DID YOU KNOW?

The sensations of flying and falling make swings one of the most popular pieces of equipment on the playground. Swinging on a playground swing allows the toddler to develop coordinated movements with the legs and body while propelling himself through the air. Although playground swings can provide a fun way to stimulate the toddler's vestibular system, adult supervision is required at all times. Researchers have found that swings are responsible for many childhood playground injuries, according to the Centers for Disease Control. Swing injuries can be serious, as they can cause traumatic brain injuries. Consider safety at all times when swings are involved.

- The toddler must want to swing; do not force the toddler to sit in a swing.
- A swing should be at a height where the toddler can easily step down and place both feet on the ground.
- Make sure the swing can support the toddler and is located away from obstacles.
- Make sure the toddler has the ability to stop the activity at any time.

Swinging movements can help the brain process and use sensory information. Participate in slow swinging activities to give the inner ear, brain, and muscles enough time to communicate with each other. As this system develops, the toddler can decide to swing faster, but let her make the choice on how fast to swing. Swinging too fast when the vestibular system is underdeveloped may cause the toddler to become dizzy and disoriented.

A swinging and rocking exercise that young toddlers enjoy is the baby glide. Sit on the floor facing the toddler, who is standing. Hold her hands and place your feet on her hips. Roll back onto the floor, and pull and

lift her into the air with your feet. Rock back and forth as you bend and straighten your legs, giving the toddler the feeling of gliding through space.

You can also rock the child using a large ball (such as an exercise or therapy ball); hold the toddler firmly around the midsection as you rock her back and forth and side to side. Rock gently and slowly at first, sometimes on her stomach, sometimes on her back, and sometimes sitting. Rock the toddler so as to place her off balance, and feel her muscles tighten in an attempt to stay on balance. As the child practices and demonstrates enjoyment of the activity, try rocking faster.

The vestibular system works all the time and not just when the toddler is off the ground swinging or rocking. Try some of these activities:

- Make an obstacle course where the toddler moves over, under, around, and through a maze of cardboard boxes and other obstacles. Each time the toddler changes levels, the vestibular system sends messages to help the child not bump into objects and remain on balance.
- Have the toddler ride a tricycle or four-wheeled vehicle, so she can practice balancing and can pedal to strengthen her leg muscles.
- Supervise while the child rides on a carousel.

Encouraging Physical Activity in Toddlers

- Place the toddler in a playground swing, making sure she is secured appropriately for her age and strength and will not fall out. Push slowly at first, and then increase the swinging speed over weeks and months as the toddler is ready.
- Let the child roll in different ways such as down a hill on grass.

BALANCE PROBLEMS—DID YOU KNOW?

It is estimated that about 35 percent of adults over the age of forty and 80 percent of adults over the age of sixty-five will at some time experience dizziness and a loss of balance because of an inner-ear vestibular disorder, and 4 percent of adults experience chronic problems with balance. A loss of balance can have a significant effect on the ability of adults and children to perform daily activities. Children are not typically screened for vestibular and balance problems. It can be difficult to determine if a young child's lack of balance is simply part of normal physical development and will improve with more experiences and practice or if a balance problem exists. Ear infections can cause toddlers to appear off balance when they are moving. If you have concerns about a toddler's balance, discuss it with a pediatrician.

Static and Dynamic Balance

Balance is commonly subdivided into two types, static and dynamic. *Static balance* is the ability to maintain a desired body posture or shape when the body is stationary. For young children, being on balance simply means not falling over. When a toddler balances on different body parts or in different body shapes, or tries to stand on one foot, he is performing static balance. *Dynamic balance* is the ability to maintain a desired body posture or position when the body is moving, starting, or stopping. When the child is skipping across the playground, walking across a beam, jumping and landing, or running to kick a ball, he is performing dynamic balance.

Both types of balance require toddlers to have control of their bodies, and working on physical activities that require balance may be difficult for many toddlers. A child needs to develop balance not only to successfully participate in a variety of physical activities but also to move safely in the home, center, and play environments. It will take time for toddlers to be able to control their movements and learn different balancing skills. Many toddlers will not seek to be off balance, so you should challenge them with balance activities that will improve their skills.

The child's success in learning how to balance will depend on his understanding that the center of gravity must be over the base of support to be on balance. A center of gravity exists in all objects, including the toddler's body, and the center shifts with movement or when weight is added. If the center of gravity is stable and not moving, the activity involves static balance. If the center of gravity is moving—as in jumping or kicking—the activity involves dynamic balance.

The base of support is the part of the body that comes into contact with the supportive surface such as the floor, balance beam, or a climbing structure on the playground. The wider the base of support, the greater the stability. When you are initially working with a toddler to develop static-balance skills, the activities should be designed to give the child a wide base of support. For example, "Can you balance on two feet and two hands?" or "Can you balance on both elbows and both knees without falling over?" In both of these examples, the toddler will have a wide base of support because he has lots of body parts in contact with the base or floor.

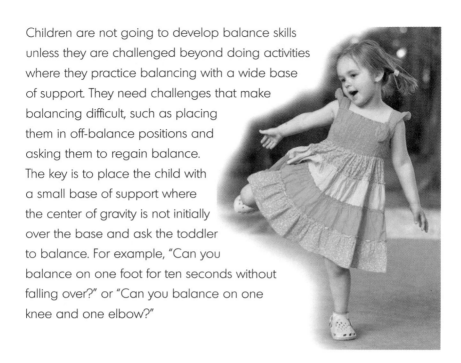

Children are not going to develop balance skills unless they are challenged beyond doing activities where they practice balancing with a wide base of support. They need challenges that make balancing difficult, such as placing them in off-balance positions and asking them to regain balance. The key is to place the child with a small base of support where the center of gravity is not initially over the base and ask the toddler to balance. For example, "Can you balance on one foot for ten seconds without falling over?" or "Can you balance on one knee and one elbow?"

Beanbag Balancing

To help toddlers begin to understand the concept of balance, show them objects that are balanced before they try to balance their bodies. A useful initial activity is to have the toddler balance a beanbag on different body parts. In doing so, she creates a visual and interactive demonstration of balance. The same rules of gravity exist with the beanbag as with the child, so the beanbag must be centered on top of the toddler's body part or it will not balance and will fall.

Children can do this activity alone, with friends in playgroups, or with family members. Give everyone a beanbag, and get started with some fun static-balance activities. Ask those participating to balance beanbags on their heads, knees, feet, backs, elbows, or foreheads. Initially, you can assist by placing the beanbag on the body part for the toddler. When you think the toddler is ready, ask her to balance a beanbag on a body part as she moves. "Can you balance the beanbag on your head while walking? on your elbow while slowly spinning in a circle? on your back while walking like a lion?"

You can purchase beanbags or make your own with the toddler's help. You can make a flat, square beanbag by cutting material into two 4-inch squares, sewing the squares together, and stuffing the bags with beans or pellets. Because beans can sprout, you may want to use lightweight plastic pellets that are heavy enough for balancing or throwing activities. Be sure the beanbags are sewn securely because the beans or pellets could be choking hazards.

Body-Part Balancing

To continue your balancing adventures, challenge the toddler to balance on many body parts with a wide base of support and then progress to a few body parts and a narrow base of support. Challenge him to hold his balance as still as possible for three to five seconds. A large hoop placed on the ground provides the toddler with a space all his own where he can balance, so have several hoops available for when friends come over. Ask the toddler to lay the hoop flat on the floor away from any obstacles. He will find it easier to concentrate on the balance activity when the task is confined to the space inside the hoop.

Wide Bases, Many Body Parts

With specific questions, prompt the toddler to try different activities:

- "Can you balance on your hands and your feet?"
- "Can you balance on two hands, two feet, and two knees?"
- "Show me that you can balance on your head, hands, and feet."
- "Can you balance on your knees and your elbows?"
- "Can you balance on your knees and one elbow?"

Narrow Bases, Few Body Parts

Use prompting questions to move to more challenging activities:

- "Show me you can balance on your head and feet."
- "Can you balance on one foot and one hand?"
- "Can you balance on one knee and one elbow?"
- "Can you balance on your head and one foot?"
- "Can you balance on one knee and one hand?"
- "Show me you can balance on your bottom. Try not to let any other part of your body touch the floor."

From these examples, you and the toddler together can design other balance challenges. Do not hesitate to ask the child if he has ideas for body-part balancing activities.

Balance-Beam Activities

Note that we are moving from static-balance activities to dynamic-balance activities—being on balance while moving. Toddlers love to walk

You may wonder when you can begin helping children do headstands. Note that most toddlers are not yet ready. Doing a headstand is a safe activity for children who possess the muscle strength and static-balance skills to perform the task. Most toddlers do not yet have enough strength and balance, however. Wait on attempting a headstand until a child has the muscular strength to do so successfully; usually they are ready sometime between the ages of four and seven.

on a balance beam (or on any object off the ground that looks like a beam), and they will frequently attempt to do so with or without adult help. Parents and caregivers know that a simple walk down the street with a toddler may turn into an Olympic challenge as the child attempts to balance on every street curb and brick wall.

A toddler needs to understand that when walking on a beam, the arms are an important part of the movement. Ask the toddler to hold her arms out "like an airplane" when walking across a beam.

Introduce the toddler to walking on balance beams placed on floor level. Make sure the toddler can easily jump or step down if she loses her balance. Children should gain skill and confidence before moving to higher beams.

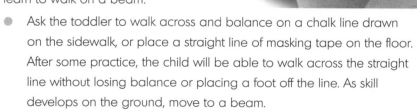

Balance beams can be expensive to purchase, but they do not have to be fancy. Lay a 1" x 4" board in the grass, and ask the toddler to walk the beam. Or simply draw a chalk line on the sidewalk, and let the child balance while walking across the line. More advanced toddlers may be ready for additional challenges such as walking across a slightly higher beam with supervision while holding a parent or caregiver's hand. You can use a sequence of challenges to help the toddler learn to walk on a beam:

● Ask the toddler to walk across and balance on a chalk line drawn on the sidewalk, or place a straight line of masking tape on the floor. After some practice, the child will be able to walk across the straight line without losing balance or placing a foot off the line. As skill develops on the ground, move to a beam.

● Have the toddler step up onto one end of the beam and walk (not slide the feet) across just as she would walk across the room. Provide guidance: "Step with one foot, and then step with the other foot."

Encouraging Physical Activity in Toddlers

Initially, the toddler may want to slide her feet across the beam, but encourage her to pick her feet up as she walks. Sliding the feet should signal to parents or caregivers that the toddler may be a little afraid to pick her feet up and walk.

- You may need to hold the toddler's hand the first couple of times to provide confidence. Stand beside the toddler, not in front, while holding one hand. Standing in front of or behind the toddler may throw her off balance. It also helps a toddler balance while walking across a beam if she holds her arms straight out at her sides. You might ask, "What do you do with your arms when you walk on a beam? That's correct; you hold your arms out like airplane wings."

- Walking sideways on a beam may be easier for many toddlers than walking forward because they can slide their feet instead of picking them up. Ask the toddler to stand on one end of the beam with her arms straight out to the side. "Pick up one foot and step sideways, then pick up the other foot and move it toward the first. Move your feet apart, together, apart, together." This is called a slide step.

Balance skills develop over time as a toddler plays and experiments with what her body can do. Help spot the toddler when she asks for help, and always be there to assist with balance when she is working at a higher level off the ground.

Jumping and Landing Skills

Some consider jumping a traveling skill, but for toddlers jumping is all about balance. Around the age of two, toddlers begin experimenting with the skill of jumping. By age three they are taking off, conducting short flights through space, and landing—sometimes several dozen times each day. During the initial stages of learning to jump, the toddler's efforts will look more like a step from one foot to the other. It takes a lot of muscular strength for the toddler to propel herself into the air.

Jumping is one of the most important foundation skills the toddler will begin to develop and is used for many purposes. Toddlers jump to express emotion, curiosity, and even frustration. Jumping is also a skill that helps toddlers get from one place to another. When children get older, jumping will help them participate in a variety of physical games and activities. Do not rush children to practice jumping; younger toddlers will not even attempt to jump. By around age two, however, most children are ready and eager to jump.

There are five basic jumping patterns:
- Two-foot takeoff to a one-foot landing
- Two-foot takeoff to a two-foot landing
- One-foot takeoff to a landing on the same foot (hop)
- One-foot takeoff to a landing on the other foot (leap)
- One-foot takeoff to a two-foot landing

Encouraging Physical Activity in Toddlers

Each of these jumping patterns requires practice to master the mature form. Initially, have the toddler practice a two-foot takeoff to a two-foot landing. This pattern is the most stable and provides a toddler with a wide base of support when landing so he will be on balance and not fall over. If he can bend the knees when taking off and landing, swing and extend arms when in flight, and successfully jump and land on two feet, staying on balance without falling, then he will have a foundation on which to build other jumping skills. The toddler will be into the preschool years before mastering the basic two-foot to two-foot pattern. Then he can try other patterns that require more muscular strength and balance to accomplish.

Jumping can be broken down into three parts:

- *Takeoff* is the action the child takes to propel his body off the ground. Takeoff always involves swinging the arms forward and upward, and bending the knees to help propel the body into the air.
- *Flight* is the action of the child's body while it is off the ground and in the air. The child can try some neat motions while in the air such as making wide, narrow, or round shapes with the hands; waving or clapping the hands; and attempting to catch or throw a ball.
- *Landing* is the action of the child's body as it reestablishes contact with the ground. Landing requires that the child bend the knees to absorb the force of landing. You can tell the child that he is really good at jumping when he can land on both feet at the same time and stay on balance.

Learning the basic two-foot takeoff to two-foot landing pattern will initially be difficult for the toddler. Starting out, a toddler does not have the strength to get all his weight off the ground. For this reason, many toddlers initially find it easier to practice jumping down from a box or step. Start

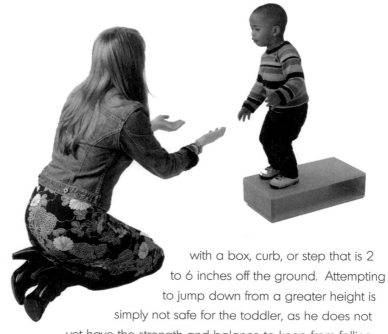

with a box, curb, or step that is 2 to 6 inches off the ground. Attempting to jump down from a greater height is simply not safe for the toddler, as he does not yet have the strength and balance to keep from falling over when landing. Initially, the jump will not be off two feet, nor will he land on two feet. Practice will look more like stepping down from one foot to the next. This is the normal progression of how toddlers begin to learn to jump. You can help by standing in front of the toddler and holding his hands, gently pushing down so that he bends his knees, then lifting the hands up and forward to help him jump down.

As the toddler gets the idea, set up the activity environment with a variety of jumping equipment. Draw chalk shapes on the sidewalk and tape lines on the ground, set up small wooden boxes, and place other small items in the jumping area to create a fun area to practice jumping. Adults will want to emphasize landing without falling over—staying on balance.

Remember that the focus on jumping and landing activities with the young toddler needs to be the basic two-foot takeoff and two-foot landing pattern. Success with this pattern will give the toddler the self-confidence to continue to develop other jumping skills. In practice, jumping is one of those skills that most toddlers naturally want to learn. As the toddler tries to get the hang of jumping, continuous supervision is required. He

Encouraging Physical Activity in Toddlers

will attempt to jump off everything! Remember that jumping is a complex movement requiring a coordination of all parts of the body. Have fun jumping with the toddler!

Riding a Tricycle

You might want to get the toddler some wheels. Ride-on toys and trikes are great for developing balance skills. Trikes also require leg strength and coordination to alternate pushing down with one foot then the other; these movements can be difficult for some toddlers. Make sure toddlers wear safety helmets and knee and elbow pads to protect them from tumbles. Set up an obstacle course for them to navigate by drawing chalk lines on the sidewalk for them to follow. Assist at first if the toddler is having trouble pushing the pedals, but don't help too much. The toddler needs to explore and learn this skill on her own. Be there for support and to help her back up when she gets stuck in a corner.

Practice with Balls

Toddlers love playing with balls, and balls provide opportunities for you to interact with the children. The best time to play is when the toddler shows interest—and for most toddlers that will be often. Think of all the fun you are going to have together rolling, throwing, catching, kicking, and striking balls.

Toddlers learn much about physical activity by exploring, experimenting, and manipulating balls. Playing with balls requires movement, and through this movement the toddler will begin to understand that physical activity provides exercise and is a lot of fun.

Unlike many of the locomotor or travel skills that develop naturally in children, ball skills will not develop on their own. They require practice and assistance from knowledgeable adults. Initial enthusiasm for playing with balls can turn into frustration if tasks are too difficult. Ball activities should initially be simple and fun but challenging enough to motivate the toddler to experiment. Adults need to assist young children in learning the fundamentals. Ball skills develop over time through continuous exposure.

With toddlers, ball play helps develop grasping skills; learning to track; and the ability to propel a ball away from the body by throwing, kicking, or striking. Toddlers are learning the properties of balls—how they bounce, roll, and move fast and slowly. Young children are interested in cause and effect, and learning how balls work certainly will help them begin to understand science concepts. Together, you can drop balls from various heights and watch how they bounce, watch as balls roll down stairs, and construct ramps around the house so the toddler can see balls roll down at different angles. The toddler is not yet ready to learn perfect technique in throwing or kicking; he simply needs to be introduced to basic ball skills and to start playing and figuring out how balls work.

Selecting the Right Types of Equipment

You will need lots of different sizes and colors of balls. A toddler will want to model what she sees adults and older children doing with balls, but she is not yet ready to be successful playing in adult-designed games with adult-sized equipment. Balls for toddlers should be constructed for toddler use—lightweight and the appropriate size for the activity. Large balls will help the toddler learn to throw and catch with two hands; throwing with one hand requires smaller balls. Provide different sizes, textures, and colors. Many toddlers still like to place things in their mouths, so make sure any ball you provide can pass a choke-tube test—it should be larger than 1¼ inches in diameter.

Make sure you have beanbags, yarn balls, foam balls, plastic balls, and rubber balls on hand. Scarves can be used for throwing and catching, and so can the toddler's favorite stuffed animal. She will select her favorite equipment and may have a different favorite each day.

Consider these tips about balls and related equipment:

- Select balls that will fit into the toddler's hands for rolling and throwing. A larger ball—8 to 10 inches in diameter—is better for catching and kicking.
- A blow-up beach ball may be easier for kicking or striking into the air.
- Beach balls are easier to catch because they move slowly through the air, allowing enough time for a toddler to get her hands and body ready to attempt a catch.
- Blow bubbles to help a toddler practice tracking skills and to practice moving the hands to catch and pop the bubbles.
- You and the toddler can have fun making your own balls. Roll up a large pair of socks to throw, or wrap masking tape around newspaper you have wadded up. Both ideas make great balls to throw at targets.

Encouraging Physical Activity in Toddlers

Provide a storage box to store all the different throwing equipment. Lightweight throwing objects can be placed in a basket and kept inside. A laundry basket works great for storage and can also be used to throw balls in. Larger balls should be placed in a box or large bag to be carried outside for kicking and striking activities. Provide a ramp or slide to roll balls up and down, traffic cones to kick balls around and for striking the ball off the top, plastic bottles for targets, a sponge bat and lightweight paddle for striking, and containers to store balls.

Unlike other physical activities where no equipment is needed, playing with balls does require a few rules. Using soft balls that will not do any damage to furniture, windows, or other objects can be great fun indoors, but larger balls are better outside or inside a large gym or multipurpose room. To a toddler, if you store a ball inside, it can be thrown inside. Keep larger, heavier balls stored outdoors, or only get them out when you go outside to play. Tell toddlers that when they use lightweight rackets or plastic bats, they need to make sure others are not close when they are swinging. Set up a few rules about not throwing objects at people or windows, and gently enforce your rules. Establishing a few simple rules now may keep parents from replacing a window when the child is seven and hits a baseball toward the neighbor's house.

Playing with balls will provide a lot of new information for the toddler to learn. Through trial and error, she will learn to calculate the speed of balls, begin to track balls as they move through the air, and learn how hard to throw or how soft to kick, depending on the situation. Avoid setting skill expectations, and simply encourage exploration. Let the toddler roll balls up and down ramps, throw them in water to see if they will float, bounce them, kick them to see how far they will go, lift them, carry them, and throw them at targets and into containers. The more exploring and ball

Most toddlers are still trying to develop balance skills when they begin playing with balls. Help the toddler with balance by providing support. Practice catching activities by asking her to sit on the floor in front of you as you roll the ball back and forth, or hold the toddler's hand to provide needed balance when she attempts to kick a ball. Select a soft outside surface such as grass to play on in case she does lose her balance. Remember that the toddler initially has little control over the direction or speed of a ball. A grass surface will slow it down and provide more opportunities for throwing and kicking. This strategy also will help the child spend less time chasing the ball when it gets away.

handling she does now, the more ready she will be to refine ball-handling skills during the preschool years.

A toddler should begin to experiment with all types of ball skills. Children typically learn the skills of kicking and throwing before they develop the fundamental movement patterns of catching, striking with hands and other body parts, and striking with implements. In practice, a toddler will work on all these skills at the same time and will learn them through repetition. For example, many toddlers can be observed picking up balls and putting them in a basket, then dumping the basket out and filling it up again. They will do this over and over. Such activities can become tedious for parents and caregivers, but this repetition is how toddlers establish a foundation of physical skills.

Rolling

A toddler will roll a ball before he throws or kicks one. Rolling a ball back and forth with a toddler is really an initial stage of developing throwing and catching skills. For some toddlers, seeing a ball flying through the air toward their face can be a scary experience. We do not want the toddler to be afraid of balls. Rolling activities help the toddler learn to track the ball and feel comfortable with an object that is slowly traveling toward him.

When you roll a ball to the toddler, he stops the ball with his hands and picks it up, practicing catching skills. Then he pushes the ball forward and rolls it back to you, which is his version of throwing. When practicing rolling activities, the toddler begins to develop the small finger muscles to grasp the ball, the eye-hand tracking skills to know when to move the hands to pick up the ball, and upper body muscles to push the ball and roll it back. In addition to working on physical development, when the toddler rolls a ball back and forth he is learning to share an object and take turns. Here are some rolling activities to try:

- You and the toddler can sit about 3 to 5 feet apart while facing each other with your legs spread. Roll a mid- to large-sized ball to the toddler, asking him to catch it and push it back to you. As he gets the idea of catching the ball and rolling it back, use different sizes and weights of balls.

- Stand up with the toddler, and bend over and roll the ball to each other. You will find that the toddler may have more difficulty stopping and catching the ball when he is standing. He may even lose his balance when trying to catch or roll the ball. It will take several months before he is fully able to roll and catch while keeping his balance.

- Ask the toddler to roll the ball under the table so you can catch it on the other side. Anytime you are able to roll the ball under an object will be great fun for the toddler. "Can you roll the ball between my legs?"

- Rolling helps a toddler begin to understand scientific concepts, such as when balls roll down ramps, the steeper the incline, the faster the ball will roll. Find natural ramps on the playground—roll a ball down a slide—or make ramps at home by placing one end of a wide board on a chair seat and the other end on the floor. Provide different sizes and shapes of balls to roll so he can experiment with which balls roll faster down the ramp. Construct ramps with different lengths and inclines.

Encouraging Physical Activity in Toddlers

Kicking

Kicking is propelling a ball or other object away from the body with the feet. Toddlers tend to walk into the ball instead of kicking it, so you initially may want to hold the child's hand to assist with balance. Once the toddler has the balance to stand on her own and kick without falling, she will want to practice kicking just about every time she goes outside, so give her a variety of kicking opportunities. When you see that she is making consistent contact with the ball, encourage her to kick for distance or kick hard. You can also encourage kicking-for-accuracy activities, but kicking for distance leads to the development of a mature kicking pattern.

- The toddler will learn a lot about kicking by watching adults and older children kick. Participate alongside the toddler so she can watch what you do.
- Toddlers will be challenged simply by making contact with a ball. Place eight to ten different-sized balls in a grassy area, and ask the toddler to kick the balls hard.

- Sometime between thirty and thirty-six months of age, a toddler will have developed the kicking skills to begin tapping the ball along the ground while moving behind it.
- Partner up and kick the ball to her, and ask that she kick it back. Most of the time, a toddler will wait until the ball stops rolling before attempting to kick it, but eventually she will be able to judge the distance and speed of the ball and will kick it back while the ball is rolling.
- Provide a toddler with a focus for kicking. Set up large targets to kick toward, such as two traffic cones 10 feet apart, or use soccer goals at a park. As skill develops, provide smaller targets to increase accuracy.

Throwing

Throwing is a basic movement pattern used to propel an object away from the body. At about eighteen months, a toddler will begin to get the hang of using his whole arm to throw a ball. All that previous practice rolling a ball will help the toddler in these initial throwing stages. He will go through a period of dropping or bouncing balls and then throwing balls underhanded before he learns how to throw overhand.

A toddler can actually begin the process of learning to throw by helping to clean up the playroom after a day of activity. Place a basket in the middle of the room, and begin picking up toys and placing them in the basket. Make a game out of this. "Let's pick up all the toys and put them in the basket." You are not throwing items in the basket at this point, but the skill of picking up an object and dropping or releasing it in a certain direction is an initial step in throwing.

You can add to this activity by placing a basket in the middle of the room and spreading beanbags out in the space. "Let's pick up the beanbags and throw them in the basket." Model a few throws, and a toddler will be on his way to gathering up the beanbags and throwing them all in the basket. When he completes the task, dump the beanbags out, and repeat the activity. Make a game out of it and see how fast you can finish. "Let's see if we can pick up all the beanbags and throw them in the basket before I complete saying the alphabet—A, B, C, D...X, Y, Z." Add to the activity by using sock balls, yarn balls, or other soft balls.

Toddlers love watching balls bounce. Using a medium-to large-sized ball, the toddler will first simply pick up the ball and drop it. As he begins to learn the properties of what a ball will do, he will raise the ball further into the air with two hands and will drop or toss it downward. Eventually he is going to raise the ball up high and throw it hard at the ground to see how high he can make the ball bounce. Beach balls are great for bouncing, as they go high and in different directions. If you are using large balls, this becomes an outdoor activity. Note that a toddler will not have the coordination to bounce a ball several times in a row until he reaches the preschool years. However, bouncing it one time, retrieving it, and bouncing again will provide hours of fun and learning.

To help stimulate a toddler to throw underhand, go outside and provide something for the child to throw into, such as a large laundry basket or a large target to throw toward. Ask him to bring his arm way back behind him and then swing the arm forward to release the ball. Don't worry about where the ball lands because a toddler has no control over accuracy at this time; he simply needs to move his arm through the underhand motion. Let the toddler select the hand he wants to use to throw, and let him switch if he wants to. In these initial stages of throwing development, he is experimenting with all the different ways the underhand throw can be

SHEET TARGETS

A toddler will enjoy helping you create a throwing target that will provide years of fun. Find a white flat sheet, and paint designs on it. Include large squares, circles, and triangles. Paint faces or other objects on the sheet so children can throw toward them. Another option is for a toddler to paint his hands and feet and then make hand prints on the sheet. Tie rope to the top corners of the sheet, and hang it between two trees or tie it to the side of a building. This is a great activity for a playgroup. If you like, you can make different target sheets with holiday themes, such as using hearts as throwing targets for Valentine's Day.

accomplished. Eventually, he will decide on a preferred hand to use. By age three, the child can begin to refine the skill with adult assistance.

At about eighteen months, a toddler will be ready to actively explore the overhand throw. He will want to throw everything he can find to see what happens as the ball travels through the air and when it lands. Provide lots of targets to give the toddler a focus for throwing, and review any rules you may have about what and where you allow throwing.

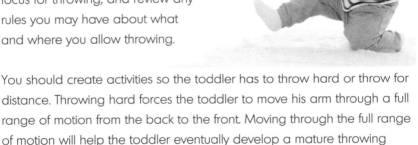

You should create activities so the toddler has to throw hard or throw for distance. Throwing hard forces the toddler to move his arm through a full range of motion from the back to the front. Moving through the full range of motion will help the toddler eventually develop a mature throwing pattern.

Targets should be large simply to provide a focus to throw toward. Trying to throw and be accurate at striking a smaller target may be frustrating to the toddler, as he will not be very good at throwing accurately until the preschool years. Don't worry if the toddler hits the large target or not,

Encouraging Physical Activity in Toddlers

practicing the throwing motion is the goal. The toddler can throw at trees, at the sky, over a rope hanging between two trees, over a playground structure, or toward a group of empty plastic bottles or milk jugs. Remind the child to throw hard. Repetition reinforces the throwing pattern and helps develop the skill, so repeat, repeat, and repeat.

Catching

Catching and striking with implements will be difficult skills for a toddler to develop. Neither skill will be fully developed until age nine to twelve. Few toddlers will be able to consistently catch a ball thrown to them until they are about three years old.

Catching is receiving and controlling an object using the body or its parts. A toddler begins to learn about catching the first time she picks up a ball off the floor and carries it around with her. The act of carrying objects around during the day is actually good practice for eventually being able to control and catch a ball. Children first catch objects with their entire body, but they eventually develop the skill to catch with only their hands. Most toddlers will hug the ball with their entire upper body instead of just using their hands to catch. Watch the toddler as she moves to grasp and pick up a large ball from the floor. She will not use just her hands but will initially wrap her whole body around it as she picks it up. This process is part of the natural progression toddlers go through in learning to catch.

Catching is a difficult skill for toddlers to develop because they have to coordinate the eyes with the hands and get their bodies in position to catch. In addition, it is natural for a toddler to protect herself initially by shying away from an oncoming object. She may even turn her body away from the oncoming ball and thereby make catching almost impossible.

As you continue to work with a toddler rolling balls back and forth, you allow her time to gather a slow-moving ball without feeling afraid that it might hit her. Rolling a ball back and forth highlights the same back-and-forth motion that the toddler will need to play catch when she is older and helps her track the ball with her eyes.

The next step in the progression is to practice catching skills with beach balls. Hold the ball in the air above the toddler, and release it for her to catch. You can also toss the ball in the air, providing even more time for the toddler to get her hands ready to catch.

Eventually, she will want to throw the ball in the air, and this would be a great throwing activity. However, most toddlers will be thirty to thirty-six months of age before they are able to control where the ball travels. When they do throw the beach ball in the air, they may not be able to track where it is moving and ready their hands for catching. If you want to work on catching skills with the toddler, you will need to drop or toss the ball to her so she has the opportunity to catch.

A toddler will also enjoy catching scarves as you drop them from above. As with the ball, hold the scarf above her head and release it. The toddler will have plenty of time to get her hands ready to catch the scarf before it touches the floor.

When the toddler is consistently catching the beach ball dropped from above her head, she is ready to practice catching a rubber ball you throw to her. You can kneel or stand a few feet away and gently throw a beach ball or toss a large rubber ball to her. Bouncing a ball to her may provide more time for the toddler to catch it. As the toddler improves her skill in catching, move farther away when throwing, and use different sizes of balls. Toddlers may not be successful all the time, but by age three, most children can catch a small ball tossed to them from 3 to 4 feet away with only their hands. They will no longer need to catch using their entire upper bodies.

Remember that throwing and catching skills do not come naturally to children, so you should model them. Don't worry about being perfect; just give the child the general idea. If you see the toddler getting frustrated,

Encouraging Physical Activity in Toddlers

stop the activity and come back and work on the skills another time. Development of throwing and catching skills requires lots of practice, so repeat activities daily.

Striking with Body Parts

Striking with body parts includes the skills of volleying and dribbling. *Volleying* is striking a ball with different body parts. For example, the toddler will begin using his hands, elbows, knees, and other body parts to strike balls. In the future, these skills can be helpful when playing sports such as volleyball, soccer, or basketball. *Dribbling* is more specific and usually refers to tapping or bouncing a ball downward with the hands, for example, in a game of basketball.

Simply making contact with the ball should be the goal of striking activities with toddlers. Activities that use striking with body parts will certainly test the toddler's skills, and most children will struggle through the preschool years to develop the eye-hand coordination needed to contact the ball. Few toddlers will be able to intentionally control the ball's flight. When the child strikes a ball, he will have no idea where it will go.

When you let children practice and experiment with striking skills, you may find that striking beach balls is a toddler's favorite activity. Making contact is the natural and basic first step in learning this new skill; however, that first step will take several years to master. You can help by introducing a variety of activities, such as striking lightweight balls in the air with the hands and with different body parts.

- Hold a beach ball or foam ball above the toddler's head, and drop it. Ask the toddler to hit the ball with one or both hands. As in many of the other fundamental skills, a mature striking pattern requires the body part to travel through a full range of motion. Ask the toddler to strike the ball hard, which will force him to bring his arm back and follow through after hitting. Don't worry about where the ball travels; the key is simply to make contact. If he has difficulty making contact, hold the ball out in front, and let the toddler strike it out of your hands until he gets the hang of striking the ball.

- Continue to drop the ball from above the toddler's head, and ask that he jump and strike it with his head. Or provide challenges such as: "Hit the ball with your elbow." "Can you raise your knee and strike the ball?" As always, these are skills that the toddler may have an easier time doing if you first model the activity.

- Stand several feet away from the toddler, and toss the ball toward him so he can strike it with his hands and other body parts. Here are a couple of secrets about striking that you should model and share with the toddler: If the ball is higher than the toddler's shoulders when making contact, he will find it easier to hold his arms straight up in the air and then move the arms in a forward and downward motion, striking the ball with the palms facing forward. But if the ball is below the shoulders, it will be easier for the toddler to strike with the palm of his hands using an upward swinging motion. One motion makes the ball travel forward, and the other makes the ball travel high in the air. You can challenge the toddler: "Hit the ball hard to see how high you can make it go."

- Play volleyball, striking the beach ball back and forth with the toddler. It is okay if the ball strikes the floor before you or the toddler strikes it back. Don't worry about rules; just keep the ball moving.

- Dribbling activities can also be done using beach balls. You should model this activity first. Hold the ball out in front of your body and bounce it to the floor. When it comes off the floor, gently tap it back down with your hands and keep it going. Toddlers at about thirty months will begin to be able to bounce the beach ball several times in a row, but children often will be in preschool before they will be successful bouncing a heavier ball.

Most toddlers will not be ready to strike heavier balls in the air. Using a ball that is too heavy too early may frustrate the toddler and turn him off to striking skills. Striking a heavy ball also can hurt a toddler's small hands. Don't push the toddler to go beyond what he is ready to do.

Striking with Implements

Most striking implements are designed for adults, and it is dangerous for toddlers to use a paddle or bat that is an official size, length, and weight. To match the child's skill level, use lightweight equipment designed for toddlers. If the toddler is using equipment that inhibits her from taking a smooth swing at the ball, then the equipment is too large or heavy and should not be used.

Striking using an implement such as a racket, paddle, bat, golf club, or hockey stick is one of the last physical skills that children will develop. These are difficult skills because toddlers and preschoolers have not yet developed mature visual-tracking skills. The toddler may demonstrate some coordination in using her hands to manipulate balls, but eye-hand coordination at greater distances from the body is more difficult. In addition, when striking a ball with implements, both the ball and the implement are usually moving at the same time. Striking a stationary object is easier than striking a moving one, so start a toddler with striking a stationary ball. Most children are eight to twelve years old before mature swinging patterns begin to emerge. The emphasis for toddlers is simply to make contact with the ball.

Most toddlers will enjoy striking activities, and certainly they should be a part of daily physical activity experiences. Your emphasis should be on helping a toddler make contact with the ball and practice moving body parts through a full range of motion. Making soft hits on a ball is a good initial activity. After a bit of practice, you can challenge the toddler to "strike the ball hard" and "see how far you can make the ball travel." That way you encourage the toddler to develop a full swinging motion with her arms and the plastic bat or paddle.

In home environments, remember that striking activities should be done outdoors. A toddler does not know where the ball is going. In her enthusiasm, she may also release the bat or paddle she is using and watch it travel across the room to break a favorite picture frame. Another safety concern when striking with implements relates to other children who may be playing. Toddler playgroups can be fun until one toddler gets hit with a paddle and is upset for the rest of the time. Make sure that when children are striking with implements, you have a large, open space without obstacles and that other children are not too close.

Striking-with-implement activities fall into three groups: striking the ball when it is on the ground, striking the ball off a tee, and striking a thrown ball. Most toddlers will be in preschool before they will be ready to successfully strike a ball thrown by an adult. The exception is that most toddlers will enjoy striking a beach ball thrown to them. Because the beach ball travels slowly through the air, a toddler has more time to get her paddle ready to attempt the strike. A smaller ball will travel too fast for most toddlers to successfully strike. Try these beginning striking activities with toddlers:

- Roll up newspaper into a stick about 1 inch in diameter and 12 inches long, and wrap the stick with masking tape. Ask the toddler to swing the stick and hit a beach ball lying on the floor. The child will have hours of fun smacking the ball with her toddler-sized bat.

- To continue to work on eye-hand coordination, try an activity where she does not strike the ball on the ground but rolls a smaller ball with her stick. Eventually she will get to hit the ball, but initially she will simply tap and roll the ball with the stick to practice making contact.

- Traffic cones for use as markers can be purchased at many toy stores. The cones range in height from 1 to 3 feet. Place a plastic ball on top of the cone, and ask the toddler to strike

Encouraging Physical Activity in Toddlers

the ball with a child-safe paddle. A cone that places the ball just below her chest height fosters successful striking. It works best to have multiple balls on hand so she can practice several times in a row before retrieving balls.

- Any soft, plastic or foam striking implement can be used to make contact with the ball and swing through a full range of motion. With the ball placed on the tee or on the ground, a toddler will have hours of fun striking balls. As she develops early striking skills, she may use one hand for a period of time and then switch and use the other. Parents should not be overly concerned about which side of the body or which hand their toddler is using. By the time toddlers become preschoolers, most have figured out which hand to use to hold a paddle. Before that time, they need to explore and experiment to see what works best for them.

- If you feel the toddler is ready for a higher-level striking challenge, you and she can both get paddles and strike a beach ball back and forth. Keep the ball on the floor at first. As the child develops more skill, you can strike the ball higher in the air.

Moving Forward

While working with toddlers to develop their physical skills, you have learned how important it is to provide time, space, equipment, and opportunities for the child to move. The toddler has spent lots of fun time with you exploring and learning about gross and fine motor skills and is beginning to understand all the things his body can do. You may think this little toddler has grown fast—and that is true—but get ready for an explosion of motor-skill development and physical growth.

During the preschool years, children grow quickly in size and strength. Development of motor skills depends on strong muscles, and muscles gain strength through repeated activity and practice. Continue to provide daily opportunities for children to participate in motor activities that require running, jumping, climbing, and balancing, as well as throwing, catching, kicking, and striking of balls. Preschool children need to be active every day to promote healthy growth, physical strength, and normal motor development.

In the next two years, a child's movements sometimes will appear skillful and consistent and at other times will appear haphazard and clumsy. It is normal for a preschool child to appear awkward and not come close to performing physical skills correctly. One day the child can kick a ball in a straight line, and the next day he falls down every time he attempts the kick. One day he can stack blocks ten high, and the next he is throwing the blocks, upset that he cannot balance more than three. This is normal; most preschool children will need years of practice to obtain the mature form of a skill. You can demonstrate patience, provide encouragement, and lend support. Welcome to physical activity and motor-skill development during the preschool years—fast paced, exciting, frustrating, challenging, and a lot of fun—all at the same time.

Expect that the preschool child will want to try a variety of new physical skills—sometimes with more eagerness and enthusiasm than skill. Increased bumps and falls will certainly occur as a preschooler pushes his motor skills to the limit. This is all a normal part of how preschool children learn about and grasp what their bodies can do. During the next couple of years, the child will discover the joys of becoming skillful at running, jumping, balancing, throwing, catching, kicking, and striking. Preschoolers will experience an explosion of learning, and you can observe and assist in this development.

Whether at school or at home, a child will benefit from a routine that provides opportunities for daily motor-skill practice. You can introduce new skills or provide information to refine and practice familiar ones. Routines that require a preschooler to assist in getting out and putting away equipment, and ones that provide repetition and sequencing of movement, will help the child make smooth transitions and better prepare him for entering school. Preschoolers learn best in all areas of development, including physical, when daily routines are created and followed.

Developmentally, three- and four-year-old children are becoming more independent. Thus, many of the strategies used with toddlers may not work or be as appropriate for preschool children. Preschool children will need more structure than they had as toddlers, but exploration and play are still equally important. All the movement exploration toddlers participated in has helped to provide a readiness to learn more during the preschool years.

Daily physical activity is more important than ever and can provide hours of fun for preschoolers. You can be a role model and offer suggestions on improving skills. Spend time each day providing planned activities and specific skill practice to assist in improving motor skills. Time for independent play becomes equally important because this is when the child can continue to practice the skill-development ideas you have provided and can explore them on his own.

Make sure the child understands how important and fun it is to be physically active. The preschool years provide a window of opportunity to develop a foundation of physical skills to be used and refined in later years. Congratulations on starting the child off on this active path! Because of your participation, the child is well on his way to becoming physically active and healthy for life.

References and Resources

American Academy of Pediatrics. 2013. *Children, Adolescents, and the Media.* Policy Statement. Elk Grove Village, IL: American Academy of Pediatrics. http://pediatrics.aappublications.org/content/132/5/958

Campbell, Denis. 2011. "Children Growing Weaker as Computers Replace Outdoor Activity." *The Guardian,* May 21. http://www.theguardian.com/society/2011/may/21/children-weaker-computers-replace-activity

Centers for Disease Control and Prevention. 2012. *Playground Injuries: Fact Sheet.* http://www.cdc.gov/HomeandRecreationalSafety/Playground-Injuries/playgroundinjuries-factsheet.htm

Choi, Ae-Na, Myeong Soo Lee, and Jung-Sook Lee. 2010. "Group Music Intervention Reduces Aggression and Improves Self-Esteem in Children with Highly Aggressive Behavior: A Pilot Controlled Trial." *Evidence-Based Complementary and Alternative Medicine* 7(2): 213–217. doi:10.1093/ecam/nem182

Copple, Carol, and Sue Bredekamp, eds. 2009. *Developmentally Appropriate Practice in Early Childhood Programs Serving Children from Birth through Age 8.* Washington, DC: National Association for the Education of Young Children.

Goodway, Jacqueline, Heather Crowe, and Phillip Ward. 2003. "Effects of Motor Skill Instruction on Fundamental Motor Skill Development." *Adapted Physical Activity Quarterly* 20: 298–314. http://www.americankinesiology.org/AcuCustom/Sitename/Documents/DocumentItem/1783.pdf

Lock, Cheryl. 2015. "Turn to the Arts to Boost Self-Esteem." *ArtsEdge,* accessed February 25, 2015. http://artsedge.kennedy-center.org/families/at-home/supporting-young-artists/what-the-arts-can-do.aspx

NASPE. 2001. *Guidelines for Facilities, Equipment, and Instructional Materials in Elementary School Physical Education.* Reston, VA: NASPE.

NASPE. 2009. *Active Start: A Statement of Physical Activity Guidelines for Children Birth to Five.* 2nd ed. Reston, VA: NASPE.

U.S. Consumer Product Safety Commission. 2014. *Public Playground Safety Checklist.* http://www.cpsc.gov/en/Safety-Education/Safety-Guides/Sports-Fitness-and-Recreation/Playground-Safety/Public-Playground-Safety-Checklist/

Encouraging Physical Activity in Toddlers

Index

Encouraging Physical Activity in Toddlers